Long Loan

This book is due for return on or before the last date shown below

St Martins Services Ltd

Tehran Rising

Tehran Rising

Iran's Challenge to the United States

Ilan Berman

ROWMAN & LITTLEFIELD PUBLISHERS, INC.
Lanham • Boulder • New York • Toronto • Oxford

ROWMAN & LITTLEFIELD PUBLISHERS, INC.

Published in the United States of America
by Rowman & Littlefield Publishers, Inc.
A wholly owned subsidary of The Rowman & Littlefield Publishing Group, Inc.
4501 Forbes Boulevard, Suite 200, Lanham, Maryland 20706
www.rowmanlittlefield.com

PO Box 317
Oxford
OX2 9RU, UK

Distributed by National Book Network

British Library Cataloguing in Publication Information Available

Library of Congress Cataloging-in-Publication Data
Berman, Ilan.
  Tehran rising : Iran's challenge to the United States / Ilan Berman.
      p. cm.
  Includes bibliographical references and index.
  ISBN 0-7425-4904-6 (alk. paper)
  1. United States—Foreign relations—Iran. 2. Iran—Foreign relations—United
States. 3. United States—Foreign relations—2001– I. Title.
  E183.8.I55B47 2005
  327.55073'09'0511—dc22   2005006727

♾™ The paper used in this publication meets the minimum requirements of
American National Standard for Information Sciences—Permanence of Paper
for Printed Library Materials, ANSI/NISO Z39.48–1992.

For Mark

With dreams of a safer and more peaceful world

Contents

Foreword

During the tumultuous 2004 presidential race, President George W. Bush and his Democratic challenger, Senator John Kerry of Massachusetts, differed drastically on a broad spectrum of domestic and international issues. For all of their disagreements, however, the two candidates unequivocally agreed on one point: The single most serious threat facing the United States is nuclear proliferation. In April of 2005, the General Assembly of the United Nations echoed this sentiment when it passed a global treaty criminalizing nuclear terrorism. Yet, as the world's leading state sponsor of terrorism rapidly approaches the nuclear threshold, the international community finds itself deeply divided.

Tehran Rising powerfully illustrates the implications of this confusion. Ilan Berman's examination of the ideology, organizing principles, and foreign policy priorities of Tehran's ruling clerics provides a telling snapshot of Iranian intentions in the post-9/11 era. His trenchant assessment of Iran's corrosive impact on the War on Terror, and of the War on Terror's impact upon Iran's place in the Persian Gulf, its nuclear ambitions, and its role in regional instability underscores that the radical regime in Tehran now constitutes one of the greatest impediments to the long-term success of American objectives in postwar Iraq and in the Middle East.

It is a challenge that the United States has neglected for far too long. In their memoirs, the Iranian radicals who famously held American diplomats hostage for 444 days from 1979 to 1981 revealed that they had originally intended to let the hostages go after only a few days but changed their minds once President Jimmy Carter made it clear that there was no danger of American intervention.

For the United States to send the same message now would be a tragic mistake. A nuclear Iran cannot be expected to follow the established doctrines of deterrence and mutually assured destruction that defined U.S. dealings with the Soviet Union during the decades of the Cold War. Rather, the expansionist nature of its Revolution, as well as its active connections to international terrorism, would make a nuclear Islamic Republic a truly global menace. At the very least, Iran's acquisition of nuclear weapons could be expected to drastically alter the terms of America's engagement in the Persian Gulf.

What is to be done? Berman proposes a twofold approach, designed to contain and delay the Iranian nuclear threat while actively promoting democratic regime change from within. It is a strategy made all the more feasible and encouraging by the recent democratic revolutions in Georgia, Ukraine, and Kyrgyzstan, and by fresh signs of political change in a historically stagnant Middle East.

Whatever course policy makers ultimately take, this much is clear: Rhetoric alone will not suffice. Armed with nuclear weapons, Iran's repressive theocracy will gain a new lease on life, emerging as an existential threat to the international community and to its own vibrant democratic opposition. *Tehran Rising* offers a sober analysis of what can be done to prevent such an outcome, why it is vital for the United States to act decisively, and what failure would mean for the United States and the global War on Terror.

It is a warning that could not be more timely.

William Schneider Jr.
Former Under Secretary of State (1982–1986)

Acknowledgments

Most books take shape over time and generate editorials and articles along the way. This one has emerged in quite the opposite way—as a distillation of three and a half years of work on Iranian foreign and security policy, encapsulated in my writings for *Defense News*, the *Jerusalem Post*, the *New York Post*, the *Journal of International Security Affairs*, and *National Review Online*, among other publications. Most directly, it is an expansion of my article entitled "How to Tame Tehran," which appeared in the spring 2004 issue of the *Middle East Quarterly*. Readers familiar with my work, therefore, are likely to find recognizable themes and arguments running through these pages. It is my sincere hope, however, that even they discover much that is new and worthwhile.

In many ways, this book is the product of numerous discussions with a broad spectrum of foreign diplomats, current and former U.S. officials, and foreign policy experts at home and abroad. Some of them I can do the service of thanking publicly. John Eubanks and Aaron Mannes, two of the most astute terrorism analysts I know, each gave me a much-needed helping hand in my exploration of Iran's connections to global instability, past and present. Michael Waller of the Institute of World Politics, my guru on all things relating to strategic communication and political warfare, did the same throughout my research on U.S. public diplomacy in the War on Terror. Jim Robbins, the National Defense University's best kept secret, was my advisor on the issue of Iran's nuclear program, as well as its likely regional (and global) effects. Two other dedicated public servants, Paul Janiczek and Howard Dickenson, helped me navigate the minefields of Beltway politics, and provided me with both support and guidance in my efforts to craft a coherent American approach toward Iran.

From Uzi Rubin, who is perhaps Israel's foremost expert on missile defense, I received not only words of encouragement, but also a crash course on Iranian missile capabilities and the potential role of missile defense in American strategy. Finally, for the past several years, Fred Cedoz has served as my political sounding board, as well as one of my closest friends. His freely dispensed insights, and his keen sense of humor, helped guide me throughout this project, as they have on so many other occasions.

Many other contributors must, by necessity, remain nameless. But I am deeply indebted to each and every one for their input, insights, and recommendations. They have profoundly shaped my thinking on Iran and the outcome of this book.

It has been my unique good fortune to find in the American Foreign Policy Council (AFPC) a home that has provided me with the resources and intellectual freedom to make this work a reality. For his unwavering support, assistance, and guidance, AFPC President Herman Pirchner has my unending gratitude.

Others at AFPC also deserve special thanks. Without the efforts of my dedicated team of researchers—Tim Agoulnik, Chris Kelley, Lisa-Marie Shanks, Catherine Drew, Marc Vogtman, and Ruth Katz—this book simply would not have been possible. Annie Earley, AFPC's communications director and all-around ballast, was always there with a kind word or a much-needed sanity check, for which I am deeply thankful. And Liz Wood, our stoic editor-at-large, was ready with stylistic suggestions and alterations that improved this work immensely.

In their day, my parents, Boris and Zina, were both refugees from the Soviet Union. They taught me from an early age about the price of freedom and the persistence of the democratic impulse. I hope this work does them proud.

Finally, I am a richer man for the constant love and patience of my wife, Hillary. Without her, little that I accomplish would be worthwhile.

Introduction:
Iran's Ascendance

On January 29, 2002, speaking to the nation in the wake of the U.S. military's successful campaign against Al-Qaeda and the Taliban in Afghanistan, President George W. Bush formally launched the current phase of the War on Terror. In the future, the president said, the United States must "prevent regimes that sponsor terror from threatening America or our friends and allies with weapons of mass destruction." In his address, he singled out three such countries: Iraq, Iran, and North Korea. "States like these, and their terrorist allies," Bush declared,

> constitute an axis of evil, arming to threaten the peace of the world. By seeking weapons of mass destruction, these regimes pose a grave and growing danger. They could provide these arms to terrorists, giving them the means to match their hatred. They could attack our allies or attempt to blackmail the United States. In any of these cases, the price of indifference would be catastrophic.[1]

More than three years later, the United States has made some progress against these threats. The campaign waged by the United States and its Coalition of the Willing in the spring of 2003 succeeded in bringing an end to Saddam Hussein's brutal regime in Iraq. Since then, despite considerable ongoing instability, the U.S.-led occupation has given way to a sovereign Iraqi government that has, however haltingly, begun assuming the trappings of responsible statehood.

North Korea, the only Asian member of the "axis," has fared better. Pyongyang's unexpected announcement of an active clandestine nuclear program in October 2002 may have spared its "Dear Leader," Kim Jong-Il, from sharing Saddam's fate. But, since then, mounting international pressure, together with a newfound consensus for containment abroad, appears at least partly to have curtailed the threat posed by the Stalinist state.

The Islamic Republic of Iran is another story entirely. Embroiled in a worldwide war on terrorism, the United States has not yet turned its attention to Tehran. Instead, it has ceded leadership to the international community on the most prominent aspect of the global threat posed by Iran: its nuclear capability. And it has remained silent on Iran's mounting adventurism in the Persian Gulf, Central Asia, and the Caucasus, as well as its persistent support for international terrorism.

For their part, Iranian leaders have begun to wake up to a startling reality. Quite suddenly, their country has become one of the biggest beneficiaries of the War on Terror. The Coalition campaign against Saddam Hussein's regime eliminated the threat posed by Tehran's most immediate military adversary, thereby cementing Iran's dominant regional standing. To Iran's east, U.S. successes against the Taliban have removed an ideological competitor for Muslim hearts and minds, while factionalism and tribal rivalries have allowed Iran to perpetuate Afghanistan's instability. Saddam Hussein's overthrow also has at least partially defanged a stubborn threat to Tehran: the *Mujahideen-e Khalq* (MKO). Since the spring of 2003, Coalition forces under a U.S.-

imposed cease-fire have curtailed the Iranian opposition group's operations in Iraq. A subsequent decree by the nascent Iraqi government has labeled the MKO, tolerated and even supported under the old Ba'athist regime, as a terrorist organization, and prompted local efforts to uproot it from Iraq.[2]

In short, by breaking up the old order in neighboring countries, the United States has given the Islamic Republic unimagined opportunities to influence the region. As Iranian policymakers are quick to point out, all the signs suggest that Iran is now destined to become the "centre of international power politics" in the post-Saddam Middle East.[3]

Iran's ayatollahs have not wasted any time putting their vision into practice. Over the past several years, their regime has mobilized massive technological, financial, and political resources as part of an ambitious campaign to dominate the greater Middle East.

In the Persian Gulf, Iran has begun to implement a new, aggressive strategic doctrine. It has launched a massive, multimillion dollar clandestine effort in Iraq aimed at radicalizing and destabilizing its western neighbor, with notable results. Iran's financial and political support has expanded the Iraqi insurgency, and allowed terrorist groups such as Hezbollah and Hamas to put down roots in the post-war political vacuum that now dominates the former Ba'athist state. Farther afield, through coercive regional diplomacy—underpinned by a massive, multiyear military rearmament—Iran has begun to tilt the Gulf's smaller, weaker states into its orbit.

At the same time, Iranian officials are busy building strategic ties to the former republics of the Soviet Union in the Caucasus and Central Asia, and forging ahead with efforts to create a regional coalition to counter American influence. In the Caspian Basin, Tehran is expanding its military capabilities, its grip on regional resources, and its efforts to prevent the countries of the "post-Soviet space" from forging relationships with the United States.

Against the backdrop of the War on Terror, Tehran has even strengthened its support for terrorism abroad. Iran has stoked the fires of the Israeli-Palestinian conflict, ratcheting up its assistance to Hamas and the Palestinian Islamic Jihad. Iran's steadfast support of Lebanon's Hezbollah has empowered the radical Shi'ite militia to bolster its global presence, as well as its influence in the Palestinian Territories. At the same time, Iran has broadened its connections to Osama Bin Laden's al-Qaeda, providing safe haven and state protection to its operatives and leaders even after September 11th.

Meanwhile, Iran's rapid nuclear advances—and its burgeoning arsenal of ballistic missiles—threaten to catastrophically alter the balance of power far beyond its immediate neighborhood.

Iran and American Strategy

Coping with Iran's growing menace will not be easy, however. For as long as it has been in existence, the Islamic Republic has bedeviled American policy makers. Almost overnight, the 1979 Islamic Revolution that swept the Ayatollah Ruhollah Khomeini and his radical brand of political Islam to power in Tehran transformed one of America's greatest allies in the Middle East into a violent, totalitarian theocracy committed to the destruction of the United States. Ever since, the U.S. has grappled with the global effects of a regime that has become the world's leading sponsor of terrorism.

Under President Jimmy Carter, the one person most often credited with "losing" Iran, official Washington vacillated between appeasement of, and diplomatic disengagement from, the newly established Islamic Republic.

Carter's successor, Ronald Reagan, took a different tack, making isolation of Iran the official policy of the United States. As part of this effort, the United States actively backed Iran's regional nemesis, Saddam Hussein, through-out the eight years of the Iran-Iraq War. But in practice, the same Reagan Doctrine that so ambitiously sought to roll back totalitarianism in the Soviet Bloc did not extend to the radical regime in Tehran. To the contrary, efforts to secure the release of American hostages in Lebanon even led Washington to embark on an ill-fated plan to secretly sell arms to Iran's ayatollahs.

The end of the Cold War and the Soviet collapse over-shadowed Iran throughout the presidency of George H. W. Bush. When the issue did reemerge, this time on President Bill Clinton's watch, Congress and the White House found themselves on opposing sides—the former committed to aggressive containment, the latter increasingly gravitating toward engagement. Quite predictably, the result was policy paralysis.

Not much has changed, even after September 11th. President George W. Bush's January 2002 inclusion of Iran in his "Axis of Evil" was a pivotal event—a modern, Middle Eastern equivalent of President Ronald Reagan's June 1982 speech before the British House of Commons, in which he had described the Soviet Union as an "Evil Empire." And among proponents of change in Iran, it sparked hopes for a more proactive approach on the part of the United States. But those dreams have since faded. Despite periodic pro-nouncements of support for the forces of democracy in Iran from the White House, inertia still remains the operating principle of American policy toward Iran.

What is clear, however, is that the United States can no longer afford the luxury of protracted inaction. Perhaps more than any other issue, the fate of Iran will dictate the direction of the Middle East. Should a reasonably moderate, pluralistic, post-totalitarian government take power in Tehran, the United States would gain a new friend in the Persian Gulf and a valuable ally in the War on Terror. But if the current Iranian regime manages to realize its strategic ambitions, the region could very well see the rise of a radical order deeply antagonistic to the United States. If that happens, there can be little doubt that America's interests in promoting democratic change and combating international terrorism will take a giant step backward.

The purpose of this book is twofold: to define the extent of the challenge Iran now poses to the United States, and to provide something that by and large has been missing, both within the U.S. government and outside it, for more than a quarter century—the makings of an American strategy toward the Islamic Republic. It is therefore divided into two parts. The first examines Iran's contemporary challenge to American security and interests in the greater Middle East. The second explores what Washington can do to contain, deter, and ultimately change the regime in Tehran.

Without a doubt, it will be one of the most challenging tasks to confront the United States in the twenty-first century.

Part I

A Gathering Threat

CHAPTER I

Terror's Source

For most Americans, the era of modern terrorism began on September 11, 2001. Before the horrific attacks in New York and Washington that day, comparatively few people in the United States understood the concept of radical political violence, particularly religiously inspired political extremism. The intermittent attacks on U.S. interests that had taken place over the preceding two decades were seen simply as sporadic manifestations of anti-American sentiment in a volatile part of the world. Worse still, over time successive administrations in Washington and the American public at large came to accept the idea that such violence was somehow part of the "cost of doing business" in the troubled Middle East.

The Islamist war against the United States did not begin on 9/11, however. It had been declared much earlier, in February 1979, when a triumphant Ayatollah Ruhollah Khomeini returned to Iran to establish the Islamic Republic. The ascendance of Khomeini's radical, anti-Western brand of Islamic revivalism transformed the Middle East, empowering a generation of Muslim radicals. And the slogan most favored by the ayatollahs, "Death to the Great Satan, America," became the universal language of Islamic insurgency. Over the years, Iran has stoked these fires, sponsoring, instigating, and inspiring a worldwide wave of terror.

The Revolutionary Imperative

Since its founding, the Islamic Republic of Iran has made the worldwide spread of its radical message a cardinal regime principle. The idea originated in the 1960s and 1970s, when the Ayatollah Khomeini languished in exile in Iraq and France. During this period, Khomeini formulated his theory about the need for radical Islamic transformation in his home country, Iran, and of "exporting" this revolution throughout the Middle East and beyond.[1] As Khomeini's brand of radical Islam rose to power in Tehran, so too did the idea that Iran's Islamic Revolution could serve as an example for other Muslim nations.

This dictum was enshrined in the preamble of the country's 1979 constitution, which announced that the Islamic Republic's armed forces "will be responsible not only for safeguarding the borders, but also for accomplishing an ideological mission, that is, the Jihad for the sake of God, as well as for struggling to open the way for the sovereignty of the Word of God throughout the world."[2] Iran's revolution occurred at the height of the Cold War, and though distinctly Muslim in nature, it also was a product of the political times. Thus, echoing the Soviet Union's attempts to foment a worldwide workers' struggle, Iran's formative document included a commitment to "unsparing support to the freedom fighters of the world" and for "just struggles . . . against the oppressors in every corner of the globe."[3]

The idea of global Islamic revolution in fact pervaded the entire governmental structure created by Khomeini following his triumphant return to Iran. It was first institutionalized by Khomeini himself, who imposed the *velayat-e faqih* (rule of the jurisprudent) as the guiding principle of the newly established Islamic Republic. Adopting the mantle of the *vali-e faqih* made Khomeini the ultimate arbiter of Iranian religion and politics, and set Iran on the course of radical religious expansionism.

4

Khomeini strengthened this priority just days after his return to Tehran by unifying the country's radical religious militias, which had been active in the overthrow of the regime of Shah Mohammed Reza Pahlavi, into the *Pasdaran* (Islamic Revolutionary Guard Corps or IRGC). Originally tasked with rooting out lingering domestic opposition to the Revolution, the *Pasdaran* quickly evolved into a clerical counterpart to Iran's conventional standing army, the *Artesh*.[4] At home, the *Pasdaran* also became tasked with organizing and training the *Basij*, a massive, radical people's militia designed to maintain social order, often by force.[5] For Khomeini, however, the principal value of the *Pasdaran* was always as a strike force capable of spreading the revolutionary message far beyond Iran's borders.[6]

It did not take long for Khomeini to put his plans into action. Just six months after his return to Iran, and with his newly formed government still struggling to consolidate its power against remnants of the pro-Shah and anti-clerical opposition, Iran's new leader had already declared the start of his modern Muslim crusade. "The governments of the world should know that Islam cannot be defeated. Islam will be victorious in all the countries of the world, and Islam and the teachings of the Koran will prevail all over the world," Khomeini announced publicly, putting the whole world on notice about his ambitions of a global Islamic order.[7]

In fact, that process had already begun. Soon after its establishment, and under the watchful eye of the *Pasdaran*, the Islamic Republic began a wide-reaching appeal to like-minded Islamic radicals from around the Middle East, North Africa, and Asia. In response, thousands of pupils flocked to Tehran, drawn by the promise of replicating Iran's successes in their own countries. There, they found military training, political assistance, and massive financial support from an Iranian government eager to internationalize its radical religious revolution.[8]

The First Front

The principal proving ground for Iran's revolutionary message became Lebanon. That country had absorbed more than a hundred thousand Palestinian refugees following Israel's declaration of independence in 1948 and the ensuing war between Israel and the combined armies of Egypt, Syria, Lebanon, Transjordan (now Jordan), and Iraq.[9] With the emergence of the Palestinian national movement in the late 1960s, the Palestinian community in Lebanon became a major base for resistance groups, including Yasser Arafat's Palestine Liberation Organization (PLO). In turn, the PLO became a principal player in the Lebanese civil war that erupted in 1974, and by the late 1970s had assumed control of much of the country's south and west with the assent of Lebanon's new overlords in Syria. Southern Lebanon became a major headache for Israeli military officials, who were forced to protect the north of their country from recurrent raids by PLO militants. By 1982, the toll on Israel's civilian population had become intolerable, and Israel launched a military invasion of southern Lebanon to quell the Palestinian attacks.

The move set off alarm bells in Syria, which had held de facto control over Lebanon since its intervention in the Lebanese civil war in 1975. Practically overnight, the regime of Hafez al-Assad in Damascus faced the prospect of losing its recently acquired puppet, a development that would definitively dash Ba'athist hopes for the creation of a "Greater Syria." The Syrian government's response was to sign a military agreement with Iran, permitting the latter to dispatch some one thousand Revolutionary Guards to arm and train the Lebanese resistance against Israel.[10] The product of Iran's involvement became evident shortly thereafter: an umbrella organization that unified elements of Lebanon's Shi'ite AMAL militia, local radical clerics, and even Islamist politicians under one roof, known as Hezbollah, the Party of God.[11]

Under Hezbollah's watchful eye, Lebanon's Beka'a Valley became a notorious terrorist hub, a place where radicals of all stripes from the world over received combat, explosives, and operational training. And as Hezbollah's notoriety grew, so did its influence, spreading from the Beka'a to Beirut, and from there throughout southern Lebanon.[12] In its day-to-day activities, Hezbollah may have focused on the struggle against Israel and the creation of an Islamic state in Lebanon, but both in dogma and in political outlook, the organization reflected the mindset of its creator and master, Tehran. As the organization's ideological platform, articulated publicly for the first time in 1985, made clear: "We view the Iranian regime as the vanguard and new nucleus of the leading Islamic State in the world. We abide by the orders of one single wise and just leadership, represented by "*Wali Faqih*" and personified by Khomeini."[13]

Hezbollah's ascendance in Lebanon marked the start of a massive wave of terror—one that, like the ambitions of the militia itself, was directed far beyond the confines of the Israeli-Arab conflict. In April 1983, Hezbollah orchestrated a truck bombing that ravaged the U.S. embassy in Beirut, Lebanon, killing sixty-three people, including seventeen Americans. Among them was Kenneth Haas, the CIA's station chief in Beirut. Just six months later, in October 1983, a similar truck bomb exploded at the U.S. Marine Corps barracks in Beirut, killing 241 Marines and wounding some 100 others. Then, in March 1984, Hezbollah operatives kidnapped—and ultimately killed—the CIA's new station chief in Beirut, William Buckley. Seven months after that, in September 1984, another Hezbollah truck bombing, this time outside the U.S. Embassy annex in Aukar, Lebanon, killed twenty-four people, including two U.S. military personnel.

These activities not only mirrored Iranian hostility toward the United States, they were actively orchestrated and supported by the Islamic Republic.[14] The casualties, in turn, took their toll on American public opinion, and by late

1984, the Reagan administration had ordered a large-scale pullout of U.S. troops. Lebanon's terrorist powerhouse and its masters in Tehran had secured a vital victory.

Beyond the Beka'a

Lebanon, however, would not be Iran's only revolutionary front. During the early 1980s, Tehran-trained radicals made abortive coup attempts in both Bahrain and the United Arab Emirates and carried out a series of bombings against Western interests in Kuwait.[15] The Islamic Republic also threw its weight behind revolutionary groups in Iraq and Saudi Arabia.[16]

The ripples from Iran's revolution spread as far as Europe. Between February and September 1986, three separate waves of bombings on the streets of Paris claimed 10 lives and sowed panic throughout France. No country was publicly implicated in the attacks, but a July 1987 report by the French internal security service, the *Direction du Surveillance du Territoire* (DST), pinned the blame on Iran.[17] The DST certainly had reason to do so: The mastermind of the attacks was discovered to be an Iranian translator by the name of Wahid Gordiji, who had been attached to the Islamic Republic's embassy in Paris. In the wake of the bombings, Gordiji took refuge at the embassy and was subsequently allowed to flee the country.[18] As it turned out, however, the French government had gotten off easy. Iranian-linked agents were also rumored to have planned, but ultimately scrapped, an attack on a French nuclear reactor, which could have killed as many as ten thousand civilians.[19]

True to its revolutionary pedigree, the Islamic Republic even extended the hand of friendship to a broad spectrum of non-Muslim radicals, including the anti-Turkish Armenian Secret Army for the Liberation of Armenia (ASALA) and the Basque separatist movement, ETA.[20] Tehran's leaders, in turn, found a receptive audience for their ideas about global struggle in the Marxist governments of Fidel Castro's Cuba and Sandinista-controlled Nicaragua, as well as the Stalinist regime of Kim Il-Sung in North Korea.[21] By the mid-1980s, less than a decade after its establishment, Iran's ayatollahs had much to smile about: their revolution had gone global.

Preserving the Revolution

Just five years later, however, the situation had changed substantially. The eruption of the Iran-Iraq War in 1980 had been a boon to Tehran, allowing the newly installed clerical regime to consolidate power at home against an external enemy. But by the time of its conclusion in August 1988, the eight-year conflict had cost the Islamic Republic dearly. Official Iranian casualties numbered close to 300,000.[22] More than half a million more had become physically or mentally disabled.[23] Industrial output had dwindled to a mere 20 to 30 percent of capacity, and estimates of economic damage ranged from $300 billion to around $1 trillion.[24] The devastating impact of the war was compounded by a major ideological crisis. In June 1989, the Islamic Republic lost its guiding light when the Ayatollah Khomeini died of a heart attack.

All this led some to hope that the wind had gone out of Iran's revolutionary sails. Surveying the Iranian political scene at the end of the war with Iraq, journalist Robin Wright concluded that Iran's revolutionary fires would dim, if not go out, over the following decade. Iran "will almost certainly have to redirect its energies, focusing less on exporting the revolution and more on domestic problems," Wright wrote in 1990.[25]

Such optimism turned out to be premature. At home, the clerical regime moved quickly to preserve power, closing ranks behind new Supreme Leader Ali Khamenei and President Ali Akbar Hashemi Rafsanjani. Both, in turn, were quick to reaffirm the centrality of "exporting the revolution" in the post-Khomeini era.

"Iran's Islamic revolution cannot be confined within borders, nations, or ethnic groups," Khamenei announced in 1989, shortly after assuming the mantle of Supreme Leader. "It is in our revolution's interest, and an essential principle, that when we speak of Islamic objectives, we address all the Muslims of the world, and when we speak of the Arrogant West, we address all the oppressors of the world."[26]

Rafsanjani, Iran's new president and an avowed regime moderate, was of the same mind. "Conditions might have changed," he would tell reporters in 1992, "but our policy has not."[27] Iran's new foreign agenda, despite some deviations in tone, would not stray far from Khomeini's principles in substance. As Muhammad-Javad Larijani, Rafsanjani's principal foreign policy advisor, put it in 1989, Iran continues to have three "vital" objectives: "The first is maintaining the Islamic nature of our regime and our status in the Islamic world. The second is defending the republic's security, and the third is expansion."[28]

Iran's ayatollahs did not stop there, however. In an effort to ensure the longevity of Khomeini's clerical government, they instituted a series of sweeping constitutional amendments centralizing even greater political power and foreign policy decision making in the post of the *vali-e faqih*, now occupied by Khamenei.[29]

Abroad, meanwhile, the Iran-Iraq War did little to mute Tehran's adventurism. The leadership in Tehran had indeed emerged from the conflict chastened, more militarily averse, and reluctant to confront regional threats directly. But Iran's ayatollahs also quickly seized upon the notion that radical proxies could serve as an attractive, low-cost substitute for direct military action, allowing Tehran to exercise control over affairs abroad despite its ravaged armed forces. Iran's revolution was, therefore, guaranteed to continue, albeit more covertly.

Against this backdrop, the collapse of the Soviet Union—and the ideological vacuum that followed Moscow's retraction from the Middle East—provided Iran with an unexpected opportunity to expand its reach and appeal in the Muslim world.

The Soviet Substitute

Tehran's troublemaking may have started during the Cold War, but it did not end with it. The dissolution of the U.S.S.R. in 1991 sidelined what had been the principal sponsor of international terror for the preceding four decades. As a result, a bevy of radical organizations in the Middle East suddenly found themselves without a patron.

Then came the first Gulf War, and with it the shattering of old illusions in the Middle East. Not only did the conflict painfully demonstrate the inadequacy of regional militaries, it also served to fragment the traditional symbols of Arab nationalism in the region—Saddam Hussein's Iraq and Hafez al-Assad's Syria. The first was discredited militarily, as Iraq's vaunted Republican Guard crumbled before U.S. and Coalition forces. The second was bankrupted politically, as Damascus joined the U.S.-led Gulf Coalition against its Ba'athist twin.

Iran was ready with an answer: its own, radical brand of Islamic revivalism. Iranian leaders dusted off plans for Islamic outreach that had been moribund since the death of the Ayatollah Khomeini in 1989. And they embraced the notion of a return to Iran's true calling—the exportation of the Revolution. As one Iranian leader put it at the time,

> What could we do in order to enter the world scene? We need a force which the enemy does not possess, and this is the force which is superior to technology and to arms. *What we need as a balancing force is the newly born, fully-alert, and ready to sacrifice Islamic force. If the Islamic Republic is supported by such a force . . . then its movement would be taken seriously.*[30] (emphasis added)

That official was none other than cleric Mohammed Khatami, then Iran's Minister of Islamic Guidance, and more recently its "reformist" president.

Iran's ayatollahs were perfectly positioned to play this role. Over the course of the Cold War, Iranian revolutionaries—along with Palestinian militiamen, Cuban Marxist radicals, and a host of other unsavory characters—had been educated in subversion, propaganda, guerrilla warfare, and anti-Western ideology in the Soviet system. Iran's Supreme Leader, the Ayatollah Ali Khamenei, is himself reportedly the product of the Kremlin's premier finishing school for third-world radicals, the notorious Patrice Lumumba University in Moscow.[31]

Iran's new status as terrorist sponsor extraordinaire was on display in February 1993, when it convened a summit of radical groups in Tehran. The meeting, organized by Iran's Intelligence Ministry, the *Pasdaran*, and the country's Supreme National Security Council, generated a game plan for global "Islamic revolutionary action." As part of this process, the Iranian regime also earmarked half a billion dollars for insurgency operations worldwide.[32]

The results were not long in coming. Islamic militants in Turkey had already taken the initiative, launching a campaign of assassinations against the country's leading journalists, authors, and secular intellectuals between 1990 and 1993. Officials in Ankara charged that the killings, carried out by a group called Islamic Action, were made possible through assistance from Iran.[33] Eight years later, a Turkish court confirmed that connection when it handed down a verdict against forty-one of the Action's members in which it declared that their terror spree had been "supported with arms and funds by the Iranians."[34] Tehran also expanded its ties to the *Partiya Karkaren Kurdistan* (PKK), building on a relationship established during the late 1980s to provide the radical Kurdish separatist group a territorial base and training for its violent insurgency campaign against Turkey.[35]

In the years that followed, this effort expanded still further:

- In Europe, Tehran's inroads were demonstrated dramatically in 1993, when three Iranian Kurdish dissidents and their translator were assassinated in Berlin by a hit team made up of Iranian and Lebanese radicals. After a three-year trial, a German court tied the assassinations directly to the upper echelons of Iran's clerical regime, including Supreme Leader Khamenei and President Rafsanjani.[36]

  Iran's activism was not limited to assassinations. Working hand in glove with Hezbollah and the Palestinian Islamic Jihad, Iran began to recruit terrorist cadres throughout Europe.[37] This effort was so successful that by 1995 the Office of Constitutional Protection, Germany's equivalent of the FBI, was charging publicly that Iran had begun a massive "political and cultural offensive" in their country.[38]

  Iranian officials even expanded contacts with the Irish Republican Army (IRA). As a result of ties forged in the early 1980s, the IRA was a prominent fixture at the global terror conference convened in Tehran in February 1993, and the Irish separatist group became an important part of Iran's planned "New Terrorist International." By the following year, the British government had taken the unprecedented step of publicly accusing Tehran of supporting and sponsoring the IRA, and had expelled the Iranian *charge d'affaires* from London.[39]
- Iran also became deeply embroiled in the Balkans. In 1991, the mounting unrest in the former nation of Yugoslavia, then in the process of fragmentation, had led the United Nations Security Council to impose a sweeping arms embargo. The move, already a controversial measure, was made all the more so as the inadequate Bosnian military began to lose ground against Serb militias controlled by strongman Slobodan Milosevic. The Clinton

administration was sympathetic to the resulting plight of the Bosnian civilian population, but stopped short of unilaterally lifting the arms embargo. It did, however, give a tacit nod to proposed Iranian arms shipments to Croatia and Bosnia.

Tehran, in turn, parlayed this opening into a major regional presence, expanding its assistance beyond simple arms supplies to the terrorist training of Bosnian Muslims and the infiltration of its intelligence operatives and agents of the *Pasdaran* into the region.[40] It also allowed Hezbollah to acquire a regional foothold, enabling it to provide critical training and indoctrination to the Bosnian *mujahideen*.[41] A subsequent Congressional investigation highlighted the scope of Iran's intrusion. "Iranian influence in Croatia," the House of Representatives report stressed, "came at the cost of endangering the safety of U.S. citizens in the region and the U.S.'s ability to work with Croatia to counter Iran's terrorist designs."[42] By 1997, the *New York Times* was reporting that Iranian elements were "mounting extensive operations" in Bosnia and had "infiltrated the American program to train the Bosnian army."[43]

- In Latin America, Iran actively assisted its terrorist proxy, Hezbollah, in expanding its already substantial international drug-trafficking and smuggling activities to the "Tri-Border" region of Argentina, Brazil, and Paraguay.[44] With Iran's help, the Lebanese militia also formed cells in Columbia and Venezuela, working through the sizeable Shi'ite Muslim communities in those countries. Hezbollah's successes led Ambassador Phillip Wilcox, then the U.S. State Department's counterterrorism czar, to dub Hezbollah "the major international terrorist threat in Latin America" in 1995 testimony before Congress.[45]

This newfound niche was demonstrated dramatically in March 1992, when Hezbollah carried out a suicide bombing against Israel's embassy in Buenos Aires,

Argentina, killing 29 and injuring 242 others. Two years later, in July 1994, the group struck again, bombing the Argentine Israel Mutual Association (known as AMIA) in Buenos Aires. Though Tehran officially denied any involvement in the AMIA bombing, which left 100 dead and more than 200 wounded, a nine-year investigation led an Argentine court in the spring of 2003 to issue international arrest warrants for five people, including Hezbollah's notorious terrorist mastermind, Imad Mughniyeh, Iranian diplomats Mohsen Rabbani and Barat Ali Balesh-Abadi, and Ali Akbar Parvaresh, a former Iranian minister and one of the founders of the *Pasdaran*.[46]

• North Africa became another theater of Iranian activity. Tehran took advantage of Saddam Hussein's defeat in the Gulf War to tighten its military and political ties to one of Baghdad's principal allies: Sudan. In December 1991 meetings with his Sudanese counterpart, Hassan al-Bashir, Iranian President Rafsanjani committed the *Pasdaran* to hosting a range of violent Islamist groups at camps located in the North African state.[47] The two countries also hammered out a deal under which Sudan would train a "nucleus for Islamic action in Europe" at a specific terror training camp outside Khartoum.[48] In the years that followed, Sudan became a haven and training center for various Iran-linked terrorist outfits, including the Abu Nidal Organization, the Algerian Armed Islamic Group (GIA) and Egypt's *Gama'a Islamiyya*.[49]

A similar effort took place in Algeria, where Iranian financing helped propel the radical Islamic Salvation Front (FIS) to a sweeping victory in preliminary parliamentary elections in 1991—a development that led to a hostile regime takeover by the country's military just a month later. That Iran had a hand in Algeria's turmoil is an understatement; not only did the Revolutionary Guards take an active role in the country's resulting civil war, they are even suspected of assassinating the country's interim president, Mohammed Boudiaf, in June 1992.[50]

In Egypt, Iranian support for two Sunni terrorist groups, the Islamic Jihad and *Gama'a Islamiyya*, underwrote a wave of terror against the regime of President Hosni Mubarak in the early 1990s.[51] Iran's activism led Mubarak, in a 1993 interview with *Time* magazine, to charge that the Islamic Republic was attempting to institute regime change in Cairo. "The Iranians have said that if they could change the Egyptian regime, they would control the whole area," he explained.[52] Iran didn't succeed, but it was not for a lack of trying; Iranian elements were subsequently implicated in the June 1995 assassination attempt on Mubarak while the Egyptian President was visiting Ethiopia.[53]

- Tehran's destabilizing influence also extended further south. In 1994, meeting with Tanzanian premier John Malecela, Rafsanjani made clear that his government was committed to helping eradicate "traces of colonialism and underdevelopment" in Africa.[54] Rafsanjani was as good as his word. In the fall of 1996, he launched a six-country diplomatic tour, visiting South Africa, Zimbabwe, Tanzania, Sudan, Uganda, and Kenya over the span of two weeks to further a radical agenda aimed at convincing the continent's Muslim population to embrace the principles of the Islamic Revolution. As part of this diplomatic offensive, Iranian intelligence officials succeeded in hammering out a cooperation pact with the radical Capetown-based People Against Gangsterism And Drugs (PAGAD), making it the "eyes and ears" of the Iranian regime in Africa in exchange for money, training, and arms.[55] In the wake of the deal, elements of Iranian intelligence and the *Pasdaran* wasted no time organizing terrorist training and mobilization for a number of indigenous Islamic movements through a variety of front groups,[56] and helping Iranian-sponsored and supported organizations such as Hamas and Hezbollah broaden their local influence.[57]

- Iran's most insidious role, however, was in the Israeli-Palestinian conflict. Tehran's direct involvement in the Israeli-Palestinian arena, although minimal during the mid- to late 1980s, expanded in earnest following the Gulf War.

In 1991, it hosted a major international conference to generate solidarity for the Palestinian cause in a radical counterpoint to the Madrid Peace Conference.[58] In its aftermath, Iran institutionalized its relationship with two terror groups. The first, the Palestinian Islamic Jihad (PIJ), had become a wholly owned subsidiary of the Islamic Republic in the Palestinian territories during the first Palestinian *intifada* in the late 1980s—similar in both structure and ideology to Tehran's principal proxy, Hezbollah.[59] The second, the Palestinian Hamas organization, had received early pledges of funding and training—promises that were codified in late 1992 under a formal agreement establishing Iranian financial and political funding for the group.[60]

These relationships were only strengthened in the years that followed. The Islamic Republic became the principal financier of the PIJ, funneling some $2 million annually to the group to bankroll its anti-Israeli activities.[61] Iran also made good on its pledges of financial support to Hamas, and began picking up some 10 percent of the group's total operational budget.[62] It also encouraged both terror outfits to develop a symbiosis with Hezbollah, helping to forge transnational partnerships that allowed them to establish military ties with—and receive military training from—the Lebanese terrorist powerhouse.[63]

To facilitate this troublemaking, the Iranian regime erected a vast domestic infrastructure dedicated to the exportation of its radical Islamic ideas. The cumulative impact of Iran's efforts was dramatic; by some estimates, 90 percent or

Tehran's Terror Machine

Pasdaran (Islamic Revolutionary Guard Corps)	A clerical analogue to the country's standing armed forces, and the Islamic Republic's principal ideological weapon. The *Pasdaran* serves as the guardian of the regime's ballistic missile and weapons of mass destruction programs, and the shock troops of the Islamic Revolution abroad. It carries out training of terrorist organizations and assists radical groups throughout the Middle East, Africa, Europe, and Asia via specialized paramilitary units, the most notorious of which is the feared Qods Force.
Ministry of Intelligence and Security (MOIS)	Iran's main intelligence agency, controlled directly by Supreme Leader Ali Khamenei. The MOIS is used domestically by Iran's ruling clergy to quash opposition and carry out espionage against suspect members of the Iranian government. It also plays a key role in planning, supporting, and carrying out terrorist operations on foreign soil, using Iranian embassies and diplomatic missions as cover.
Ministry of Foreign Affairs	One of the main enablers of the Iranian regime's international terrorist presence. Agents of the *Pasdaran* and MOIS often operate out of Iranian missions abroad, where they are stationed under diplomatic cover, complete with blanket diplomatic immunity. These agents – and through them Iranian foreign proxies – use the Ministry's auspices to untraceably obtain financing, weapons, and intelligence from Tehran.
Ministry of Culture and Guidance	Facilitates *Pasdaran* infiltration of – and terrorist recruitment within – local Muslim populations in foreign nations via diplomatic missions and free-standing cultural centers. The Ministry is particularly influential in majority Muslim countries, including many of the former Soviet Republics. Between 1982 and 1992, the official in charge of the Ministry – and of its role in support of Iranian terror abroad – was Mohammed Khatami, Iran's future "reformist" president.
Basij	The Iranian regime's premier tool of domestic terror. The *Basij* is used by the ayatollahs to quell domestic anti-regime protests and eradicate "un-Islamic" behavior. The Basij also plays an important supporting role in Iran's state sponsorship of terror, training militants from groups such as Hezbollah and Hamas for guerrilla warfare.
Guruh-i fishar	Internal vigilante or "pressure" groups harnessed by the Iranian government. Though officially independent, these domestic paramilitaries actually operate under the patronage of government officials, the *Pasdaran* or the MOIS, targeting internal opposition to the clerical regime.
Bonyads	Massive cartels overseen by Iran's Supreme Leader. The *bonyads* serve as financial conduits for the Islamic Republic's terrorist cause of choice. The sums controlled by these organs are enormous, accounting for between 10 and 20 percent of Iranian national GDP. While many of their functions are legitimate, they are also used by Iran's ayatollahs to funnel money to their pet causes, from funding domestic repression to arming terrorist groups abroad.
Proxies	As Iran's role in international terrorism has grown more sophisticated, it has increasingly relied on terrorist proxies to promote its radical agenda. The Islamic Republic today helps to sustain an array of militant surrogates, ranging in ideology from the radical Islamist to the secular nationalist.

Sources: Michael Eisenstadt, *Iranian Military Power: Capabilities and Intentions* (Washington: Washington Institute for Near East Policy, 1996); Mohammad Mohaddessin, *Islamic Fundamentalism: The New Global Threat* (Washington: Seven Locks Press, 1993); Michael Rubin, *Into the Shadows: Radical Vigilantes in Khatami's Iran* (Washington: Washington Institute for Near East Policy, 2001); Paul Klebnikov, "Millionaire Mullahs," *Forbes*, July 21, 2003.

more of the major acts of global terrorism committed in the two decades before September 11th can be traced back to Tehran.[64]

Iran versus the War on Terror

Less than a month after the terrorist attacks on New York and Washington, President George W. Bush addressed the nation to announce the formal commencement of military operations in Afghanistan. The president used the occasion to level an ultimatum at the international community. "Today we focus on Afghanistan, but the battle is broader," Bush declared in his televised address. "Every nation has a choice to make. In this conflict, there is no neutral ground."[65]

Iran has made its choice. Testifying before Congress in early 2002, then-CIA Director George Tenet observed that there was "little sign" Iran had scaled back its sponsorship of terrorism.[66] Tenet's remarks were a distinct understatement. Not only has Iran maintained its links to international terror, since September 11th it has dramatically increased them. In the process, Iran's ayatollahs have succeeded in unleashing a new wave of global instability.

Expanding Hezbollah's Horizons

More than two decades after its creation, Hezbollah remains Iran's principal proxy. Since at least the mid-1990s, U.S. officials have estimated that Iran provides Hezbollah with approximately $100 million annually, as well as maintaining a contingent of *Pasdaran* forces in Lebanon to coordinate Tehran's contacts with the Shi'ite militia.[67] After September 11th however, that support has been bolstered by a number of new strategic initiatives, all designed to expand the group's regional profile and strategic reach.

Iran, with active assistance from Syria, has launched a massive effort to broaden the Lebanese militia's missile capabilities—one that has included the delivery of thousands of Katyusha artillery rockets, as well as hundreds of Iranian-made *Fajr-5* short-range missiles, to the terrorist group.[68] This program has been wildly successful; Israeli intelligence now estimates that Hezbollah has approximately 13,000 short-range rockets, some 500 medium-range rockets, and several dozen longer-range rockets with a range of up to 215 kilometers (130 miles).[69] Moreover, these capabilities have profoundly altered the correlation of forces between the Shi'ite militia and the State of Israel. In a January 2004 interview with Israel's *Channel 2* television, one prominent Israeli parliamentarian cited Hezbollah's expanding arsenal—and its resulting ability to target much of Israel—as the reason why Israel so far has failed to take military action against the group.[70]

Tehran also has actively aided and abetted the group's efforts to acquire weapons of mass destruction. In mid-2002, reports emerged that Hezbollah had started to outfit its arsenal of short-range missiles with chemical warheads at two terrorist training facilities run by Iran's *Pasdaran*.[71]

Since September 11th, Iran has worked hard to ensure the survivability of its most important terrorist asset. Fearing that Hezbollah might become the target of American military action, it redirected some of the militia's activities to Africa in late 2001.[72] There, drawing on its vast smuggling network and its involvement in the African diamond trade, the organization has thrived. The extent of Hezbollah's successes became evident in late 2003, when the crash of a commercial charter jet bound for Beirut from Benin killed three Hezbollah officials, reportedly carrying some $2 million in what amounts to regular contributions to the group from Lebanese expatriates.[73]

Furthermore, in early 2004, Iranian Defense Minister Ali Shamkhani made a high-profile visit to Syria, where he signed a "memorandum of understanding" codifying Iran's commitment to defend the Ba'athist state in the event of an Israeli or American offensive. On a subsequent stopover in Beirut, Shamkhani made a point of meeting with Hezbollah's top leadership, to whom he affirmed that the newly minted security guarantees between Tehran and Damascus also extended to the terrorist group's stronghold, Lebanon.[74]

Iran's assistance, in turn, has allowed Hezbollah to commence a landmark strategic expansion, widening its presence in Europe, Asia, Latin America, and the Levant.[75] The group has also deepened its alliances with other terrorist organizations, helping elements of al-Qaeda to put down roots in Lebanon, assisting Hamas with the development of an indigenous missile capability, and coordinating anti-Israeli and anti-American activities with an assortment of extremist groups.[76] As a result, according to American officials, the threat to American security posed by Hezbollah now rivals, or even exceeds, that of al-Qaeda.[77]

The Iran–Al-Qaeda Connection

Though they received little attention at the time, Iran's links to al-Qaeda broke into the public eye in October 2000, when Ali Mohamed pled guilty for his role in the 1998 bombings of the American embassies in Nairobi, Kenya, and Dar es Salaam, Tanzania. In his sworn testimony in U.S. federal court, the Egyptian-born Mohamed, an American citizen and retired U.S. Army officer, revealed that he had served as a trainer for key al-Qaeda lieutenants, and as the point man for the Bin Laden network in Africa. He also outlined links between al-Qaeda and the Iranian-sponsored Hezbollah dating back to the early 1990s, when Iran used the Lebanese Shi'ite militia to provide explosives training to al-Qaeda and to Egypt's *al-Jihad* organization.[78]

Mohamed's revelations shed light upon a long-standing operational partnership. According to the definitive final report of the National Commission on Terrorist Attacks upon the United States, better known as the 9/11 Commission, Iran and al-Qaeda forged an informal accord in late 1991 or 1992, under which al-Qaeda *mujahideen* traveled first to Iran and then to Lebanon's Beka'a Valley to receive explosives training.[79] Subsequently, in 1995 and again in 1996, Bin Laden operatives approached Tehran directly, offering a bilateral anti-American partnership to Iran's intelligence ministry.[80] And in July 1996, when Iran's clerics convened a major terrorist summit in Tehran, representatives from al-Qaeda—as well as delegates from the anti-Turkish PKK, the Palestinian Islamic Jihad, Hezbollah, and the Popular Front for the Liberation of Palestine—reportedly turned out to support Iran's plans for a *terrorist internationale* aimed at the United States.[81] At various times throughout the 1990s, Bin Laden's right-hand man, Ayman al-Zawahiri, is also said to have traveled to Iran, where he was hosted by the country's Minister of Intelligence and Security, Ali Fallahian, and by Ahmad Validi, the Islamic Republic's chief of terrorist operations.[82]

The tactical alliance forged between al-Qaeda and the Iranian regime during the 1990s has only been strengthened by the War on Terror. In the months after the terrorist attacks of September 11, 2001, Iran became an important transit point for al-Qaeda fighters *en route* to the war in Afghanistan, as well as a safe haven for dozens of the group's irregulars fleeing Coalition forces.[83] This collusion led the White House to publicly warn Iran against harboring al-Qaeda in August of 2002.[84]

These public admonitions, however, did little to dampen the Iran–al-Qaeda connection. Since the destruction of al-Qaeda's traditional safe haven in Afghanistan, Iran appears to have emerged as an important base of operations for the terror network. In October of 2003, reports surfaced that high-level members of al-Qaeda—including Saad Bin Laden, one of Osama Bin Laden's oldest sons; al-Qaeda operations chief Saif al-Adel; and Abdullah Ahmed Abdullah, the organization's chief financial officer at the time—had begun to coordinate the organization's global activities from Iran, where they were operating under the active protection of the *Pasdaran*.[85] It is believed that this cell was responsible for planning and coordinating the terrorist bombings that killed 34 people in Riyadh, Saudi Arabia, in May of 2003.[86]

Iran has also bolstered its partnership with al-Qaeda's affiliates. Hundreds of fighters from the organization's radical Kurdish branch, *Ansar al-Islam*, have reportedly found their way to Iran's Kurdish-dominated western regions since being ousted from Iraq in the spring and summer of 2003 as part of Operation Iraqi Freedom. There, they have begun a new campaign—to radicalize the Islamic Republic's strongly secular Kurdish population—with Tehran's active support.[87] Iran similarly has developed an intimate relationship with Ahmad Fadil Nazal al-Khalayleh, better known as the notorious Jordanian terrorist Abu Musab al-Zarqawi. A member of the Sunni Muslim Brotherhood, Zarqawi became affiliated with al-Qaeda in 2000, when he established a terrorist training camp for Jordanians in Afghanistan and—in the process—opened up a new terrorist transit route through Iran.[88] From these auspicious beginnings, Zarqawi built an extensive terrorist network based in Iran, which became the hub for radical operations in neighboring Iraq and throughout the Middle East.[89] Since the start of the Iraq war, Zarqawi has assumed a central role in the ongoing insurgency against Coalition forces, and Iran's ayatollahs have played an important role in his troublemaking, allowing him and affiliated terrorists to freely enter and exit Iranian territory.[90] Moreover, Zarqawi apparently received temporary safe haven in Iran during the Coalition's April 2004 offensive in Fallujah, where he visited training camps run by the *Pasdaran* and obtained logistical support for ongoing terrorist operations from the *Pasdaran*'s Qods Force.[91]

Co-opting the Israeli-Palestinian Conflict

In January 2002, Israeli naval forces carried out a daring interdiction of a Palestinian freighter, the *Karine-A*, on its way to the Gaza Strip. What they found was astounding; upward of fifty tons of Iranian arms—including anti-tank grenades and short-range Katyusha rockets—destined for the Palestinian Authority.[92] Just four months later, in May 2002, another Israeli seizure netted a similar cache of Katyusha rockets, anti-aircraft missiles, anti-tank ammunition, and mortars aboard the Syrian-flagged *Santorini*. The ship had been part of regular arms deliveries to Gaza from Lebanon, this time orchestrated indirectly by Iran, together with Syria, through Hezbollah and the Popular Front for the Liberation of Palestine-General Command (PFLP-GC).[93] The two interdictions shed light on Iran's rapidly expanding footprint in the Palestinian Territories, where Tehran has begun to alter the character of the long-running Israeli-Palestinian conflict.

Since the outbreak of the second *intifada* in September 2000, Iran has assumed a leading role in the Palestinian insurgency against Israel, funneling both arms and money to a number of terrorist organizations active in the West Bank and Gaza Strip. The *Karine-A* and the *Santorini* were early manifestations of this assistance. They have since been supplemented by more assertive Iranian efforts.

Via Hezbollah, Tehran has begun a takeover of Palestinian terrorist groups. Using Iranian and Lebanese funds, Hezbollah has begun to co-opt secular nationalist terrorist groups previously loyal to the Palestinian Authority, such as the Al Aqsa Martyrs Brigade, a radical offshoot of the PLO's chief political faction, the *Fatah* party.[94] Simultaneously, the group has strengthened its hold on the West Bank and Gaza Strip through the establishment of independent, autonomous terrorist cells and the creation of an elaborate smuggling network designed to arm its growing cadres. This strategy, carried out under the direction of Iran's

Ministry of Intelligence and Security (MOIS) and *Pasdaran*, is dramatically expanding Hezbollah's presence within the crumbling Palestinian Authority.[95] According to the estimates of Israel's Shin Bet internal security service, the Lebanese Shi'ite militia directed over fifty separate Palestinian terror cells in 2004—a seven-fold increase since 2002.[96]

Iran has also broadened its grip on radical Islamist groups active in the West Bank and Gaza Strip. In the summer of 2002, it convened a meeting of leading Palestinian terrorist groups in Tehran at a summit presided over by Interior Minister Ali Akbar Mohtashemi, widely known as the "midwife" of Hezbollah for his role in creating the Lebanese militia. The gathering drew Palestinian Islamic Jihad (PIJ) leader Ramadan Abdallah Shallah, as well as delegates from Hamas, Ahmed Jibril's PFLP-GC, and the Palestinian Authority. Iran's Supreme Leader, Ali Khamenei, used the occasion to announce that the PIJ's operational budget, previously channeled via Hezbollah, henceforth would be administered directly by Tehran, and that Iran's financial allocations to the group would be expanded by 70 percent to help the terror group ramp up its anti-Israeli activities.[97]

Iran's expanding brokerage of PIJ has been matched by its growing control over Hamas. Under pressure from Tehran, Hamas and Hezbollah, long competitors for influence in the West Bank and Gaza, mended fences in mid-2001.[98] Since then, Hamas' fortunes have declined dramatically; between late 2003 and early 2004 alone, an Israeli campaign of targeted assassinations eliminated three key Hamas leaders, including the organization's architect, Sheikh Ahmed Yassin.[99] This has led Hamas to recognize Hezbollah's primacy. In March 2004, Khaled Misha'al, the head of Hamas' political wing, signed an unexpected strategic accord with Hezbollah chief Hassan Nasrallah expanding cooperation between their two organizations.[100]

Since then, Hezbollah's influence—and Iranian ideology—has become so influential within the organization that the Sunni Hamas, a member of the Muslim Brotherhood, took the rare step in the summer of 2004 of speaking out on non-Palestinian issues, throwing its support behind the radical Shi'ite cleric Muqtada al-Sadr and his resistance to Coalition forces in Iraq. According to Israeli terrorism expert Reuven Paz, this uncharacteristic move is a manifestation of "increasing Iranian influence in the Palestinian arena, inside and outside of Palestine."[101]

Iran's assistance also has played an important part in cobbling together a loose-knit coalition of these terror groups. Since mid-2001, Hamas, Hezbollah, PIJ, the Al-Aqsa Martyrs Brigades, and other *Fatah* factions, despite their disparate political agendas, have demonstrated a growing coordination of activities, sharing weapons and intelligence, and even carrying out joint operations.[102]

At the same time, Iran has moved decisively to fill the niche once occupied by Saddam Hussein as a financier of Palestinian suicide bombing. In the summer of 2003, reports began to emerge that Iran was offering $50,000 to the families of Palestinian suicide bombers—double the sum that had been paid by Saddam when he was in power.[103] Iran is also responsible for directly soliciting terrorist attacks on Israel. Between August 2002 and 2003, Tehran is said to have sponsored at least fifteen terrorist attacks against Israel, both within Israel and against Israeli troops and civilians in the West Bank and Gaza.[104]

The results of Iran's strategic offensive have been dramatic. Directly and through its proxies, the Islamic Republic has virtually monopolized the Palestinian resistance. Influential Israeli investigative reporter Ehud Ya'ari estimates that Iran, working through Hezbollah, is responsible for "no less than 80 percent" of the most recent violence in the second Palestinian *intifada*.[105] Israeli officials agree; according to them, Iran is now "in control of terrorism in Israel."[106]

If anything, Iran's influence has become even more pervasive in the Palestinian Territories since the death of Yasser

Arafat in November 2004. The political vacuum that has emerged in the West Bank and Gaza Strip in the wake of Arafat's passing has created an opening for even greater Iranian involvement and influence. In a sign of things to come, Farouk Qaddoumi, Arafat's successor as head of the PLO's *Fatah* faction, visited Tehran in December 2004 for a series of meetings with top Iranian officials, with the goal of "consolidating relations between the Iranian and Palestinian nations."[107] As part of these efforts, Palestinian officials have welcomed Iranian "infiltration," dubbing it a positive manifestation of Tehran's support for "the Palestinian people and the Palestinian cause and the liberation of Palestine."[108]

Target: America

"Death to America is not a slogan. Death to America is a policy, a strategy and a vision." So declared Sheikh Hassan Nasrallah, the spiritual leader of Hezbollah, on the organization's popular *Al-Manar* television station in the midst of the U.S.-led campaign in Iraq.[109]

Nasrallah's words are more than empty rhetoric. Launched over two decades ago, the covert war against the United States and its interests abroad waged by Iran and its proxies is hardly a thing of the past. In fact, in the midst of the War on Terror, Tehran's radical campaign has entered a new and frightening phase.

Signs of this new activism are everywhere. In the summer of 2004, the Islamic Republic took the unprecedented step of establishing the world's first publicly advertised training facility for suicide bombers. Run by the *Pasdaran*, the center is designed to provide assistance to insurgency groups operating out of Tehran, as well as to recruit "martyrs" for attacks against Israel and Coalition forces in Iraq. The success of this effort has been unprecedented; just weeks after its establishment, thousands of volunteers had reportedly already enlisted in the unit, dubbed the Committee for the

Commemoration of Martyrs of the Global Islamic Campaign.[110]

Furthermore, this activity is not localized to the Middle East. The summer of 2004 offered a glimpse of Tehran's infiltration of the United States, when two Iranian "diplomats," ostensibly attached to the Islamic Republic's mission to the United Nations, were caught and deported by New York City authorities for casing and photographing sensitive transportation and infrastructure sites in Manhattan. The arrests marked the third seizure of its kind in just two years.[111]

The ideological marching orders for this and other acts of sabotage and intelligence gathering had been proclaimed at Tehran's Al-Hussein University in May of 2004. "We have a strategy drawn up for the destruction of Anglo-Saxon civilization and for the uprooting of the Americans and the English," Hassan Abbassi, a high-ranking *Pasdaran* official and a leading advisor to Iranian Supreme Leader Ali Khamenei, had announced. "The global infidel front is a front against Allah and the Muslims, and we must make use of everything we have at hand to strike at this front, by means of our suicide operations or by means of our missiles. There are 29 sensitive sites in the U.S. and in the West. We have already spied on these sites and we know how we are going to attack them."[112]

Abbassi's call to arms must be taken seriously. Four months prior to his address, Iran held a major international summit of terrorist groups as part of celebrations commemorating the twenty-fifth anniversary of events surrounding the 1979 Islamic Revolution. The forum provided representatives from Hamas, the Palestinian Islamic Jihad, and al-Qaeda affiliates like *Ansar al-Islam*, as well as seventeen international branches of the Iranian-sponsored Hezbollah, the opportunity to coordinate a common strategy against the United States and its allies.[113] The message is clear, and it is one of profound importance for the United States and its allies in the War on Terror. In the words of Ayatollah Ahmad Janati, head of Iran's powerful Guardian Council, "Today, mankind has a common enemy, and that enemy is the American Great Satan. Anyone who fights the Great Satan for whatever reason is on our side, and anyone who does not is on the opposite side."[114]

CHAPTER **2**

The Real "Islamic Bomb"

On August 14, 2002, the National Council of Resistance of Iran (NCRI) convened an impromptu press conference at the posh Willard Intercontinental Hotel in Washington, DC. The briefing was sure to be controversial. The NCRI, an umbrella group of Iranian opposition parties, had become *personae non grata* in Washington in 1997, when the Clinton administration, seeking to curry favor with the new, "reformist" president in Tehran, had designated its chief member, the *Mujahideen-e Khalq* (MKO), a Foreign Terrorist Organization under U.S. law.

The August gathering, however, was a bombshell even by Beltway standards. Surrounded by representatives from some forty news outlets, NCRI representative Alireza Jafarizadeh disclosed alarming new details of Iran's nuclear plans. The Islamic Republic, Jafarizadeh said, had embarked on a clandestine nuclear program of unprecedented scope, one that was home to at least two previously unknown nuclear sites: a clandestine research and nuclear fuel facility in Natanz, Kashan province, and a heavy-water plant in Arak in central Iran.[1] These stunning revelations jolted the post-9/11 world awake to a new threat: Tehran's all-out quest for nuclear capabilities, and the frightening specter of a nuclear Iran.

Iran's nuclear ambitions, in fact, had been a source of mounting American concern for years. During the 1990s, officials in Washington had watched with growing alarm as Iran's accelerating quest for weapons of mass destruction (WMD) prompted it to ratchet up its atomic contacts with a host of foreign enablers. In May 1995, then-Secretary of State Warren Christopher publicly expressed these fears when he warned of a dual-track Iranian nuclear program, encompassing both uranium and plutonium enrichment, and fueled by foreign support.[2] Christopher's warnings were echoed by his successor, Madeleine Albright, who on more than one occasion urged Russia and European nations to scale back their atomic assistance to the Islamic Republic.[3] The Bush administration inherited these concerns, and made curbing proliferation to Iran a major tenet of its pre-9/11 foreign policy agenda.

The U.S. was not alone in its fears. Officials in some corners of Europe broke with the continental consensus regarding the need to engage Tehran. These politicians expressed similar worries over Tehran's pursuit of WMD, and formally pledged cooperation with the U.S. in denying Iran's atomic efforts.[4] On the whole, however, Iran's nuclear program would not receive the international attention it deserved until the NCRI's fall 2002 disclosure shed light on the true scope of Tehran's atomic effort—and the nuclear ambitions of its rulers.

Since then, a series of discoveries by the International Atomic Energy Agency (IAEA)—ranging from advanced clandestine nuclear development to the presence of trace weapons-grade uranium—and reluctant disclosures by Iranian officials themselves, have unearthed an atomic endeavor dramatically broader and more mature than originally believed.

There are two routes to a nuclear capability: highly-enriched uranium and plutonium. Tehran is pursuing both. It is doing so through numerous facilities, some open and some secret, but all part of what one Iranian opposition figure has likened to a clerical "Manhattan Project."[5]

Tehran's Path to the Bomb

Though the current crisis over Iran's nuclear program is comparatively new, Iran's atomic effort itself is not. It dates back at least to the early 1970s, when, at the initiative of the Shah Mohammed Reza Pahlavi, Tehran launched an ambitious national program to develop nuclear energy.

Pahlavi's elaborate plans included the construction of a nationwide grid of some twenty-three nuclear power plants.[6] But they created few ripples, either in Europe or in the United States. The Shah had made his intentions clear from the outset, and Iran had ratified the Nuclear Nonproliferation Treaty (NPT) in 1970, just two years after its inception. Moreover, the Pahlavi regime, for all of its shortcomings, was rightly seen in the West as reasonably moderate and accountable. Officials in Europe and the U.S. therefore concluded that, on balance, they would not lose any sleep over the Shah's atomic quest.

The Islamic Revolution of 1979 changed everything. Early on, the radical clerical movement that overthrew the Shah extended its antagonism of all things Western to the old regime's nuclear plans, and work on the Iranian atomic program ground to a halt. But the moratorium did not last long; Tehran's nuclear drive again took center stage with the outbreak of hostilities between Iran and neighboring Iraq. By 1987, Iranian officials were publicly intoning the importance of their country's nuclear effort, as well as its predominantly strategic applications.[7] And Iran matched its words with action. During the 1980s, it gradually resumed uranium processing and the construction of new nuclear weapons research facilities, even going so far as to formalize an agreement with Pakistan on atomic cooperation.[8] By the end of the Iran-Iraq War, the country's atomic effort largely had been reconstituted—this time, with a clearly military objective.

Iran's nuclear endeavor survived the end of hostilities with Iraq. By the late 1980s, the Iranian regime—under the direction

of its new leader, President Ali Akhbar Hashemi Rafsanjani—
had expanded and intensified its nuclear development.
Officials in Tehran made diplomatic overtures about atomic
cooperation to a number of countries, including Argentina
and India, and succeeded in acquiring "yellowcake" uranium from South Africa in 1988–1989.[9] They also held preliminary discussions on nuclear cooperation with officials in
Moscow during this period.[10] The Iranian regime even built
upon China's eagerness to build a "new global order" to
counteract American supremacy abroad, codifying nuclear
accords with Beijing in 1989, and again in 1991.[11]

Iran's quest accelerated dramatically after the Soviet collapse. The outbreak of the first Persian Gulf War in January
1991 riveted Iran's ayatollahs, who saw proof of Washington's
overwhelming military superiority in the rapid dismantlement
of the Iraqi military. But the Gulf War held another lesson as
well; the February 25, 1991, Scud missile attack by Baghdad
on Coalition forces, an attack that killed twenty-seven U.S.
servicemen, exposed America's "Achilles Heel"—a serious
potential vulnerability to unconventional attack. It also reinforced to Iranian officials a cardinal post–Cold War priority:
the need for weapons of mass destruction, the means to
deliver them, and the will to use them.

The implosion of the Soviet sphere, meanwhile, made
such weapons readily available. For decades, the Soviet
Union had kept an iron grip over its vast nuclear infrastructure through multiple, overlapping safeguards such as
guarded frontiers and numerous isolated atomic stockpiles.
But the economic turmoil that rocked Russia after the Soviet
collapse jeopardized these safety measures, making nuclear
materiel vulnerable to theft. And with widespread crime,
economic malaise, and corruption, there was no shortage of
takers.[12]

Tehran took these developments to heart. In 1994, it
began negotiations with at least one nuclear facility in the
former Soviet republic of Kazakhstan regarding the purchase

of fissile material. The failed effort would be confirmed two years later by Kazakhstan's ambassador to the United States, who disclosed to the *Washington Times* that "Iran had attempted to buy unidentified materials from a major Soviet nuclear facility in his country."[13] Also in 1994, Iran's clerical shock troops, the *Pasdaran*, made a similar bid in the Russian Federation. Operating under the moniker of the "Islamic Jihad Organization," *Pasdaran* elements attempted, unsuccessfully, to buy an atomic bomb or fissile material from one of Russia's crumbling nuclear cities.[14]

The failure of these overtures, however, was more than compensated for by Tehran's booming atomic trade. By the mid-1990s, Iran's quest for the bomb was being assisted by a host of foreign suppliers.

Russia quickly emerged as Iran's principal nuclear ally. Building on a series of nuclear protocols signed in the late 1980s and early 1990s, Moscow and Tehran put in motion the plan for a Russian reactor at the southern Iranian city of Bushehr.[15] The agreement, when it was finally concluded over American objections in January 1995, committed Russia to the construction of a 1,000-megawatt nuclear reactor. At about the same time, Russian Atomic Energy Minister Victor Mikhailov pledged to provide Iran with critical atomic know-how—authorizing the training of hundreds of Iranian scientists and technicians in complex nuclear processes.[16]

Despite repeated assurances that this cooperation was strictly "civilian" and "peaceful" in nature, Russian politicians made no secret of its strategic implications. In a mid-1995 interview, Mikhailov characterized the nuclear ties between Moscow and Tehran as the "trump card" in the Kremlin's foreign policy.[17] And signs quickly surfaced that Russian cooperation extended far beyond Bushehr. Just five years later, American officials were speaking publicly about a robust Russian-Iranian nuclear agenda—one that included "research reactors, heavy-water production technology, and laser-isotope separation technology for enriching uranium."[18]

If Russia helped revive Iran's nuclear ambitions, China sustained them. As early as 1992, Rafsanjani had visited Beijing and obtained a Chinese commitment to supply the Islamic Republic with a 300-megawatt nuclear power reactor.[19] This understanding spawned a series of subsequent WMD deals, and by 1996 the Pentagon had officially designated China as a "principal supplier of nuclear technology to Iran."[20]

Faced with mounting diplomatic and economic pressure from Washington, Chinese President Jiang Zemin formally pledged to conclude "no new nuclear contracts" with Iran in October 1997.[21] Beijing's good behavior did not last long, however; just three months later, the U.S. discovered and averted the commercial sale of nuclear-related chemicals to an Iranian atomic facility by a Chinese firm.[22] A little over a year after that, a U.S. intelligence report revealed that China had "revived" talks with Iran regarding the possibility of constructing a graphite production facility within the Islamic Republic—one capable of producing some two hundred tons of nuclear-grade graphite annually.[23]

Iran's nuclear cooperation with North Korea progressed more quietly. During the early 1990s, Pyongyang was itself under growing pressure from the U.S. for its nuclear program. As a result, the North Korean leadership was careful to keep its atomic trade with Tehran a closely-guarded regime secret. Nevertheless, some telltale signs did leak out; press reports in South Korea and the Arab world, for example, disclosed that General Myong-Rok, Commander of the North Korean Air Force, had inked an agreement on nuclear cooperation as part of an official visit to Tehran in February 1994.[24] The following year, a prominent Iranian expert revealed that North Korea had helped Iran build several secret atomic facilities, including sites housing two nuclear reactors.[25]

Pyongyang's nuclear partnership with Iran's ayatollahs was echoed in another corner of Asia. Shortly after taking office in 1989, Rafsanjani's effort to expand Iran's nuclear suppliers had taken him to Islamabad, where he was rumored to have codified a new security pact to provide Iran with nuclear assistance.[26] The deal resulted in a broad atomic partnership—one that endured throughout the 1990s and included Pakistan's provision of key technical designs and advanced atomic technology.[27]

Thus, on the eve of 9/11, Iran had already managed to cobble together an ambitious national effort to develop nuclear weapons.

Iran's Atomic Archipelago

Four years later, the results are staggering. Although exact details are understandably sketchy, Iran's effort to acquire the bomb appears today to be massive, encompassing close to two dozen strategic sites scattered throughout the country.

Natanz, approximately two hundred miles south of Tehran, houses a previously clandestine underground uranium enrichment facility overseen by Iran's Supreme National Security Council, the Islamic Republic's chief security policy arm. The facility, now in the process of expansion, is ultimately expected to be capable of producing enough highly enriched uranium for fifteen to twenty nuclear weapons annually.[28]

Arak, approximately 150 miles south of Tehran, is the location of a heavy-water production plant. Like the Natanz site, its existence was a closely guarded secret until it was revealed by the NCRI in August 2002. Subsequently, in March 2003, the Iranian government announced plans to build a heavy-water reactor at the Arak site.[29] The spent fuel from this facility could be reprocessed to create weapons-grade plutonium.

Bushehr, in southern Iran, is the public face of the Iranian nuclear program. Construction of the 1,000-megawatt plutonium reactor built there by Russia was completed in October 2004.[30] American officials fear that, once "hot," the reactor will be capable of generating weapons-grade plutonium, and could provide the Islamic Republic with critical know-how that would be used in the production of nuclear weapons.

The central Iranian city of *Isfahan* is believed to be the core of the Islamic Republic's nuclear weapons program. It is the site of four separate nuclear reactors, as well as a uranium conversion facility essential to the regime's efforts to develop highly enriched uranium.[31]

Tehran, Iran's capital, is home to a small five-megawatt research reactor located at the Tehran Nuclear Research Center in the suburb of Amirabad, and to the Kalaye Electric Company, a weapons manufacturer that has been implicated in uranium conversion experiments and the production of centrifuge components. In February 2003, the NCRI also revealed that two nuclear labs, satellites of the large uranium enrichment plant at Natanz, were housed in the city's suburbs.[32] Subsequently, in November 2004, the group disclosed details of an additional nuclear weapons research facility, overseen by the Iranian Ministry of Defense, housed in Tehran's Lavizan district.[33]

Parchin, thirty kilometers southeast of the Iranian capital, is said to be the site of a clandestine military complex that has been carrying out uranium enrichment work since the year 2000. Its existence was disclosed by the NCRI in November 2004.[34]

Saghand, in the eastern province of Yazd, is the site of a massive uranium mine estimated to be capable of producing one hundred twenty thousand tons of uranium ore annually for the next two decades.[35] In February 2003, the Iranian government announced that it was preparing to mine the Saghand site.[36]

A related processing facility at *Ardakan*, in central Iran, turns uranium ore into "yellowcake"—enriched uranium concentrate—which is then refined still further to be weapons usable.[37]

Another "yellowcake" production plant, located near the southern Iranian port city of *Bandar Abbas*, is expected to come online by early 2006.[38]

Mo'allem Kaleyeh, a mountain facility in northern Iran, is suspected of housing uranium enrichment gas centrifuges. Inspections by the IAEA in early 2004 uncovered traces of uranium at the Kalayeh facility.[39]

Bonab, located in northwestern Iran, is the site of the Bonab Atomic Energy Research Center. That facility, though ostensibly for agricultural and medicinal research, is suspected of housing a nuclear enrichment capability.[40]

Neka, on Iran's Caspian coast, is believed to house a key underground nuclear weapons site, complete with two 400-megawatt reactors acquired from Russia under a secret 1995 deal.[41]

Chalus, also situated on Iran's Caspian coast, is reportedly home to an underground nuclear weapons facility staffed by foreign specialists.[42]

Another atomic military facility, run by the *Pasdaran*, is alleged to exist at *Darkhovin* in southern Iran.[43]

Kaleteh, between Shahrud and Damghan in central Iran, is rumored to house an underground nuclear reactor built with North Korean assistance.[44]

A similar clandestine nuclear reactor is said to exist in the desert near *Tabas* in Iran's eastern province of Khorasan, at a site targeted by Iraq during the Iran-Iraq War.[45]

Fasa, near Shiraz in Iran's Fars province, is believed to be the location of a Chinese-built uranium hexafluoride plant constructed as part of the 1991 nuclear accord between Beijing and Tehran.[46]

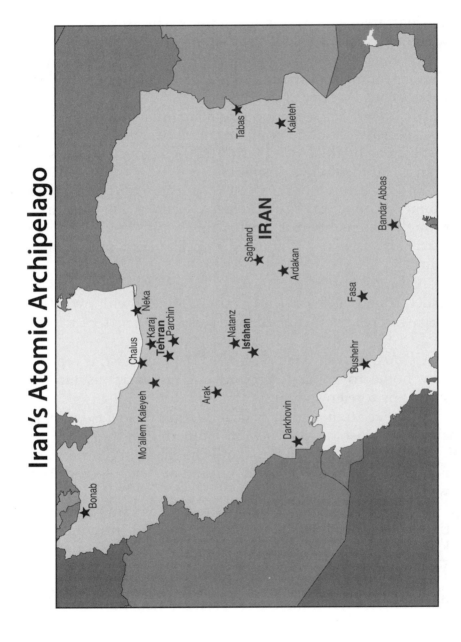

Iran's Atomic Archipelago

In addition to civilian nuclear research facilities, *Karaj* in northern Iran also reportedly houses a secret nuclear weapons site constructed in the mid-1990s with the help of Chinese experts.[47]

Ominously, these publicly known facilities could be just the tip of the iceberg. Officials in Washington strongly believe that other, clandestine atomic sites now exist within Iran. This fear has been fanned by Iranian officials, who have publicly hinted in the wake of the NCRI's 2002 revelations that still-undiscovered nuclear facilities essential to Iran's nuclear program operate within their country.[48]

Learning to Love the Bomb

Given the scope of this effort, it is tempting to think that Iranian opinion is settled on the subject of atomic power. In fact, however, at least some Iranians actually appear to be deeply ambivalent about the idea of a nuclear capability, based on the understanding that such a move could lead to serious international consequences.[49] But among the Iranian leadership, any debate over the prudence of "going nuclear" was settled long ago—and settled in favor of moving forward.

These strategic calculations have been reinforced by the experiences of the other members of President George W. Bush's "Axis of Evil." The spring 2003 military campaign against Saddam Hussein's regime was carried out on Iran's western border, and it was watched closely from Tehran. What Iranian officials saw convinced them of the prudence of nuclearization. Over the span of just three weeks, U.S. military forces drove deep into Iraq, crushing Saddam Hussein's vaunted Republican Guard, and systematically dismantling those Iraqi forces that had not turned tail and fled. Attacks from Iraq's feared weapons of mass destruction also failed to materialize (while subsequent searches for these weapons have turned up empty).

Iraq's implosion was deeply demoralizing to the Iranian leadership. The conventional war-fighting capability of Saddam Hussein's regime was known to have far outstripped that of Iran, and its unseemly collapse did little to dispel Iranian fears of overwhelming American military power. "The fact that Saddam was toppled in twenty-one days is something that should concern all countries in the region," one Iranian official told the Reuters news agency in the wake of Saddam's ouster.[50]

North Korea, by contrast, had fared much better. In October 2002, it stunned the United States and the international community when it revealed an active clandestine nuclear program. For much of the preceding decade, the prevailing wisdom in Washington and abroad had been that Pyongyang was in compliance with the grand bargain it had struck with the Clinton administration in 1994. Under that deal, dubbed the "Agreed Framework," North Korea had pledged to freeze its nuclear development in exchange for an annual allotment of half a million tons of heavy fuel oil from the U.S. (to compensate for energy lost as a result of its ostensibly "civilian" nuclear program). To sweeten the pot, officials in Washington also cobbled together an international consortium to provide North Korea with two light-water nuclear reactors.[51]

In the process, they encountered prescient warnings from regional experts, who suggested Pyongyang did not view its multi-decade nuclear effort as a bargaining chip, but rather saw it as a staple of regime survival.[52] Officials in the American national security establishment, however, relied heavily on the durability of their deal with Pyongyang, and failed to put any serious safeguards or verification mechanisms in place. So, by the time Pyongyang made its atomic announcement in October 2002, Kim Jong-Il's regime had had eight years to covertly perfect its nuclear capabilities.

For Tehran's leaders, North Korea's nuclear breakout— and the subsequent success Pyongyang has had in deadlock-ing American diplomacy on the Korean Peninsula—has only reinforced the prudence of their own atomic endeavor. Given American successes so far in Iraq, the North Korean experience is an important object lesson: the key to preempting U.S. strategy lies in the acquisition of weapons of mass destruction. In the words of one Western diplomat: "Iranian leaders got together after the Iraq war and decided that the reason North Korea was not attacked was because it has the bomb. Iraq was attacked because it did not."[53] It's no wonder that, in their discussions with their North Korean counterparts, Iranian officials have made a point of stressing their admiration for Pyongyang's policies, as Foreign Minister Kamal Kharrazi did when he lauded Kim Jong-Il's ability to withstand American "pressure, hegemony and superiority" to North Korean Deputy Foreign Minister Kim Yong-Il in Tehran in December 2003.[54]

For this reason, Iranians in government, regardless of their political stripes, have rallied around the idea of their country as a nuclear power. As Mostafa Tajzadeh, a player in Iran's reformist parliamentary faction, told the *Washington Post* in the midst of Operation Iraqi Freedom, Iran's nuclear effort is "basically a matter of equilibrium. If I don't have a nuclear bomb, I don't have security."[55]

The Mullahs' Waiting Game

Ever since the NCRI's August 2002 bombshell, world attention has been riveted on Iran's nuclear ambitions.

The UN's nuclear watchdog, the IAEA, was the first to spring into action. In February 2003, a team led by IAEA Director-General Mohammed ElBaradei visited the Islamic Republic. This fact-finding mission, however, only served to confirm international concerns; ElBaradei and his team of experts uncovered unmistakable signs of centrifuge activity in direct violation of Iran's commitments under the Nuclear

Nonproliferation Treaty (NPT).[56] The discoveries led the IAEA to issue a June 2003 status report that declared Iran to be in breach of its "obligations under the Safeguards Agreement with respect to the reporting of nuclear material, the subsequent processing and use of that material and the declaration of facilities where the material was stored and processed."[57]

The IAEA's mounting criticism led to pressure from other quarters, including the Group of Eight (G-8) and the European Union (EU). Rebukes from both international bodies were followed by a fresh criticism from the IAEA, which urged Iran to "adhere strictly to its obligations" under the NPT in a late November 2003 board resolution.[58] Since then, mounting international concern, and growing calls for Iranian nuclear transparency, has continued.

Through it all, Iran has engaged in a game of high-stakes cat-and-mouse with the international community over its nuclear program. In October 2003, it struck a deal with France, Germany, and Great Britain to suspend its uranium enrichment activities, only to renege on the agreement just eight months later, in June 2004.[59] The temporary halt in the regime's uranium program subsequently announced by Hassan Rowhani, Secretary of Iran's Supreme National Security Council, has also fallen by the wayside. In September 2004, Iran declared plans to begin processing thirty-seven tons of "yellowcake"—enough to produce up to five nuclear weapons.[60] Tehran has also managed to circumvent its December 2003 decision to sign on to the Additional Protocol to the NPT, which permits snap inspections and invasive monitoring of segments of its nuclear sector by the IAEA. And it has begun to "sanitize," move, and otherwise hide suspect sites from international inspectors, preventing effective oversight of its nuclear efforts.[61] As these moves have made clear, Tehran continues to pursue a strategy designed to delay, obfuscate and otherwise derail international intervention until it is capable of "going nuclear."

Exactly how soon that could happen is the subject of some debate. According to the U.S. intelligence community, a nuclear Iran is unlikely until somewhat later this decade.[62] Other nations, however, believe that an Iranian bomb could materialize much sooner. In January 2005, Major-General Aharon Ze'evi, the head of Israel's military intelligence, warned that Iran was six months from enriching uranium. "Iran is not currently capable of enriching uranium to build a nuclear bomb, but it is only half a year away from achieving such independent capability, if it is not stopped by the West," Ze'evi disclosed in a public address at Haifa University.[63] Based on these projections, Israeli intelligence officials now believe an offensive Iranian nuclear capability could emerge by 2007.[64] But if these estimates are off, even by a few months, Iran could present the world with a nuclear fait accompli.

Iran's ayatollahs have every reason to believe they will eventually succeed in doing so. For one thing, international consensus on the issue of Iran's nuclear program is unlikely. In dealing with Tehran, policy makers in Europe have consistently gravitated to economic and diplomatic engagement, while American officials have preferred containment and isolation. These are more than simple differences in style; they reflect fundamentally contrasting ways of coping with Iran's rogue behavior.

For another, the pressure the international community could bring to bear, even if it had a mind to do so, would be insufficient to blunt Iran's nuclear aspirations. Since two of Iran's main atomic suppliers, Russia and China, wield veto power on the UN Security Council, any application of sanctions or—even more seriously—authorization of military force in response to Iran's nuclear violations remains highly improbable.[65] And the UN is even less likely to tackle the true reason why a nuclear Iran would be a global menace: the character of the radical regime in Tehran.

A Proliferation Nightmare

In May 1998, India stunned the world when, over the course of three days, it detonated five atomic devices outside the town of Pokhran in the northern state of Rajasthan. Less than a month later, India's dramatic emergence from the nuclear closet was answered by a series of Pakistani atomic tests in a nuclear tit-for-tat that marked a dangerous escalation of the long-running regional rivalry between the two countries.

Although it was carried out in response to India, Pakistan's nuclearization reverberated throughout the Muslim world. For decades, and particularly since Israel's emergence as the region's sole presumed nuclear power in the late 1960s, officials throughout the Middle East had dreamed of an "Islamic bomb" that would help them achieve parity with Israel and the United States. Islamabad's nuclear breakout was therefore greeted as the dawn of a new era of Islamic empowerment. "Pakistan's possession of nuclear power is to be considered an asset to the Arab and Muslim nations," the late Sheikh Ahmed Yassin, the spiritual leader of the Palestinian Hamas terrorist organization, told the Kuwaiti daily *Al-Rai Al-Aam*.[66] In Syria, the state-owned *Al-Thawrah* newspaper took up the call, and—in a reflection of its government's own nuclear ambitions—dubbed Pakistan's nuclear development to be the right of every country desiring "security, rights, and sovereignty."[67]

Iranian officials went even further. Foreign Minister Kamal Kharrazi became the first foreign dignitary to visit Islamabad after Pakistan's nuclear breakout, where he lauded then-Prime Minister Nawaz Sharif for the latter's achievement, saying he had "strengthened the confidence of the Moslem world."[68] Within the Islamic Republic, meanwhile, the event became a major cause for celebration, with Iran's top jurist, the Ayatollah Mohammad Yazdi, publicly feting Pakistan's newfound nuclear capability as a way to achieve "equilibrium with Israel" at the tomb of the Ayatollah Ruhollah Khomeini.[69]

Pakistan's nuclear breakout also captured the imagination of another regional player, Osama Bin Laden. Immediately following the Pakistani nuclear tests, the al-Qaeda leader issued a communiqué entitled "The Nuclear Bomb of Islam," in which he declared that "it is the duty of the Muslims to prepare as much force as possible to terrorize the enemies of God."[70]

So far, however, such a capability does not appear to have materialized. To be sure, Pakistan's nuclear progress—and its subsequent, determined work on ballistic missiles—has added a new and dangerous dimension to the decades-long Indo-Pakistani stand-off in South Asia. Recently uncovered evidence of a rogue nuclear cartel run by none other than the father of Pakistan's atomic bomb, Abdul Qadeer Khan, also suggests that a number of nations—among them Libya, Iran, and Syria—have in fact benefited from Islamabad's new status. And at least a portion of this activity has almost certainly been conducted with the knowledge and acquiescence, if not the outright approval, of the Pakistani government. But a larger "nuclearization" of the Muslim world still remains a hope rather than a reality.

All of that may be about to change. In the hands of Iran's ayatollahs, an atomic capability could become a dangerous export commodity. After all, Iran's chemical, biological, and nuclear weapons programs are already in the hands of its clerical army, the *Pasdaran*.[71] So is the Islamic Republic's burgeoning ballistic missile arsenal.[72] Since the *Pasdaran* is the regime's principal point of contact with terrorist groups like Hezbollah and Hamas, the possibility that Iran's nuclear and ballistic missile advances could therefore translate into substantial terrorist gains must be considered.

In fact, signs of just this sort of activity have already begun to emerge. During the summer of 2002, at the height of the Palestinian *intifada* against Israel, Western intelligence sources disclosed that Iran had launched a $150 million program to arm and train terrorist groups active in Lebanon. As part of this initiative, Tehran boosted shipments of Iranian-made *Fajr-5* short-range missiles to proxy groups like Hezbollah, and launched a comprehensive program to train Hezbollah guerrillas and Palestinian militants in the use of the 70-kilometer range rockets.[73] In tandem with this assistance, Iran also increased its artillery supplies to its Lebanese proxy, delivering thousands of *Katyusha* rockets to Hezbollah via Syria.[74]

Subsequently, in the fall of 2002, Iranian missile proliferation took a still more ominous turn, when a leading British newspaper revealed that "Iranian forces" in Lebanon had acquired and deployed units of Tehran's *Zelzal-2* missile. The disclosure marked an important milestone: with the 150-kilometer-range rockets, Iran for the first time gained the capacity to strike major urban centers in Israel by proxy. Commenting on the news, an Israeli intelligence expert assessed that Iran had "changed the strategic balance and limited Israeli military options."[75]

The rationale for Iran's proliferation was clear. At least in some quarters, it was seen as an important insurance policy for Tehran, giving Iran's ayatollahs the ability to activate a "northern front" against Israel if the American-led offensive against Iraq ever became a threat to their own regime.

Moreover, Iran's proliferation activities have not been limited to the Israeli-Palestinian arena. Tehran increasingly is following the lead of another rogue—North Korea. Pyongyang is already the world's premier proliferator, selling ballistic missiles and WMD technology to states throughout the Middle East, Africa, and Asia. According to an October 2003 report from the South Korean Defense Ministry, proliferation is the single largest source of revenue for the Stalinist state, with missile sales to the Middle East in 2002 alone accounting for at least $60 million in revenue.[76] Iran has begun to do the same, becoming a major provider of missile and WMD technology to a number of weapons-hungry states.

Libya has been one such client. Over the past several years, the American intelligence community has expressed growing worries about the expanding WMD partnership between Tehran and Tripoli. Testifying before the Senate Armed Services Committee in March 2002, Admiral Thomas Wilson, then the director of the Pentagon's dedicated intelligence arm, the Defense Intelligence Agency, warned that Iran was "beginning to proliferate missile production technologies" to a number of client states, including Libya.[77] Wilson was not alone; the same day, in separate testimony to the Senate Foreign Relations Committee, Carl Ford, the State Department's Assistant Secretary for Intelligence and Research, warned publicly of Iran's growing potential for "secondary proliferation."[78]

These burgeoning links broke into the public eye in February 2002, when a leading Arabic-language daily disclosed that Iran had agreed to build a medium-range missile plant in Libya.[79] Only months later, Iran reportedly inked an unprecedented $13.5 billion ballistic missile and WMD cooperation agreement with the Libyan government. As part of the deal, the Islamic Republic promised to provide Iranian experts to train the Libyan military in the maintenance and combat use of Iranian missiles, as well as to provide chemical warheads for Tripoli's arsenal of extended range Scud-class missiles.[80]

In turn, when Libyan strongman Muammar Qaddafi unexpectedly had a change of heart regarding his pursuit of weapons of mass destruction and ballistic missiles in late 2003 in response to British and American pressure, the regime in Tehran moved quickly to prevent incriminating disclosures about its own clandestine nuclear weapons effort. Iran threatened to launch a guerrilla campaign against Libya using extremists from Libya's banned Combat Islamic Group (GICL), which have been trained and shielded within Iran by the *Pasdaran* since September 11th.[81] Tehran's carrot and stick approach—stepping up support and training for the group, while simultaneously pledging to restrict its activities, provided Libya refrains from divulging details of Iran's WMD efforts—has been effective. So far, Qaddafi has remained mum about his country's WMD ties to Iran's ayatollahs.

Iran has also stepped up WMD cooperation with another rogue state: Bashar al-Assad's Syria. Since the start of the War on Terror, Damascus has significantly accelerated its work on ballistic missiles and weapons of mass destruction. This has included efforts to extend the range of its arsenal of *Scud* missiles, as well as outfitting its medium-range ballistic missiles with chemical warheads.[82] Iran, for its part, has been quick to lend a helping hand. In 2002 alone, Tehran was responsible for transferring both solid- and liquid-fuel technologies to the Ba'athist state, and helping it to establish an indigenous missile production plant.[83]

Iran's assistance has done wonders. By mid-2003, senior officials in Jerusalem were estimating that the regime of Bashar Assad had at least 100 ballistic missiles equipped with the nerve agent VX targeting central Israel, and that Syrian leaders, who for years have attempted to achieve strategic parity with Israel, had "achieved their aim of balancing Israel's nuclear advantage."[84]

The Stakes

Over time, Iran's nuclear program has become a source of deep concern for policy makers in Washington, and preventing an Iranian nuclear breakout is now a top strategic priority for the United States. President George W. Bush himself has gone so far as to warn publicly that Washington "will not tolerate" a nuclear-armed Iran.[85]

The reasons for apprehension are clear. Iran's nuclear advances will spur a dangerous regional domino effect, accelerating the efforts of neighboring states to acquire atomic status. In fact, the beginnings of such efforts can already be seen; in October 2003, the *Washington Times* revealed details of a secret agreement recently concluded between Saudi Arabia and Pakistan granting Riyadh access to Pakistani nuclear technologies in exchange for cheap, steady supplies of Saudi crude.[86] The news was a public confirmation that the House of Saud—despite all the recent talk of better relations between Tehran and Riyadh—has begun to actively contemplate the need for a strategic deterrent against Iran.

Other countries can be expected to follow Saudi Arabia's lead. Turkey, historically a strategic competitor of Iran, is somewhat insulated from the Iranian nuclear threat, both as a result of its membership in NATO and because of the policies of Ankara's Islamist AKP government, which has put a premium on better ties with Tehran. Nevertheless, lingering uncertainty over its place among the European community of nations might just prompt Turkey to pursue a nuclear option of its own.[87] Egypt, in turn, might do the same, spurred by worries over parity with Iran and eager for the opportunity to match Israeli WMD capabilities. In fact, recent discoveries of plutonium traces at Egyptian nuclear facilities—and rumors that Cairo might have gained nuclear technology and know-how from Libya's now-defunct nuclear program—have deepened international suspicions about the nuclear aspirations of the government of Egyptian President Hosni Mubarak.[88] Even the new government in Iraq, fearful of the leverage over local and regional politics wielded by a nuclear Iran, might be tempted to respond in kind. The ability of the U.S. to control such impulses on the part of regional states would be far from absolute, and would require costly investments in regional security structures and a major reconfiguration of military deployments to the Middle East.[89]

Additionally, American officials can expect a nuclear Iran to drastically alter U.S. strategic calculations in the Persian Gulf. Armed with nuclear weapons, Iran will have the ability to threaten American troops operating to its east and west, in Afghanistan and in Iraq. But this kind of nuclear threat would do more than simply hold U.S. and allied troops at risk. As U.S. intelligence officials make clear, Tehran's ongoing military rearmament—and its resulting strategic control of the Strait of Hormuz—already gives it the power to control a substantial portion of the oil trade from the Persian Gulf.[90] An atomic arsenal would make this situation much worse, and empower Iran's clerics to use nuclear blackmail to virtually dictate energy terms to Europe and the United States.

Iran's substantial leverage over the smaller, weaker countries of the Persian Gulf would also increase dramatically. The collapse of the Clinton administration's "dual containment" policy in the mid-1990s effectively removed the American strategic umbrella from the countries of the Persian Gulf. Ever since, these states have had to seek some sort of an accommodation with Iran's ayatollahs. This drift would only be accentuated by an Iranian nuclear capability, which would decisively establish Tehran's regional dominance. Over time, the U.S. will find the already problematic Persian Gulf less and less hospitable, as regional states eschew contacts with Washington in favor of a *modus vivendi* with a nuclear-armed Tehran.

Iran's capacity for troublemaking is also poised to grow exponentially. Acquisition of a nuclear capability can be expected to embolden Iranian support for terrorism as a strategic tool. "With a nuclear weapons option acting as a deterrent to U.S. and allied action against it," a recent study by a leading Washington think tank concluded, "Iran would likely lend greater support to terrorists operating against Israel, Iraq, Libya, Saudi Arabia, Europe and the U.S."[91] By the same token, a nuclear Iran is bound to feel itself more free to promote its radical revolutionary principles abroad, and to assume an even greater role in the current insurgencies in Iraq and Afghanistan, not to mention the Israeli-Palestinian conflict. The United States, deeply enmeshed in the Middle East as part of its global War on Terror, can ill afford any of these eventualities.

Yet, as grave as it is, the challenge of a nuclear Iran represents only part of a substantially larger picture. In tandem with its nuclear advances, Iran's ayatollahs have embarked upon an ambitious strategic agenda designed to make their regime the center of gravity in the post–Saddam Hussein Middle East.

CHAPTER 3

Suddenly a Superpower

In the spring of 2002, as momentum gathered in Washington for a military campaign against Saddam Hussein's regime in Iraq, the U.S. intelligence community made an unexpected announcement. Testifying before the Senate Armed Services Committee about emerging threats to American security, Defense Intelligence Agency Director Thomas Wilson issued an unexpected warning. "Iran's navy," Wilson disclosed, "is the most capable in the region and, even with the presence of Western forces, can probably stem the flow of oil from the Gulf for brief periods by employing a layered force of KILO submarines, missile patrol boats, naval mines, and sea and shore-based anti-ship cruise missiles."[1]

Wilson's warning underscored a remarkable development. For much of the 1990s, Iran had been relegated to the margins of Middle Eastern politics. Operation Desert Storm had not ended with Saddam Hussein's overthrow, as many had hoped. But in its aftermath, the first Bush administration cobbled together a regional strategy designed to "contain" Iraq's dictator. When the Clinton administration took office in 1992, it expanded this containment to include the Islamic Republic. And, despite some deficiencies, this policy, dubbed "dual containment," held at first. Though Iran's ayatollahs had begun a major national effort to reconstruct their country's armed forces almost immediately after the end of the Iran-Iraq War, these attempts—when surveyed in the late

1990s—had not made much headway, thanks in large part to American efforts to isolate and sideline the Islamic Republic.[2]

Yet on the eve of Operation Iraqi Freedom, Iran had reemerged as a major regional player. Through its military rearmament, it had begun to redraw the balance of power in the Persian Gulf. There were new signs of vibrant strategic cooperation with WMD supplier states like Russia, China, and North Korea, and officials in Tehran were articulating an increasingly ambitious, expansionist foreign policy line in the Middle East. Most of all, Iran's ayatollahs, whose regime had been tottering toward collapse just a few years earlier, had become convinced that their country was destined for regional hegemony.

Iran's Return

The reason for this dramatic turnaround was simple. Iran's economy, heavily pegged to the price of oil, had been devastated by declining world energy prices during the mid- to late-1990s. Crude had started the decade at $36 per barrel, buoyed by the political instability that accompanied the first Persian Gulf War. By early 1998, that figure had plummeted to under $15 per barrel.[3] Dependent on oil for almost 25 percent of gross domestic product and more than 80 percent of export earnings,[4] Iran was left facing economic ruin.

Then, everything changed. A confluence of economic factors, ranging from the East Asian economic crisis to Russia's August 1998 fiscal meltdown, led to a sharp increase in world energy prices. By the year 2000, exchange prices of close to $30 a barrel had given Iran an unexpected economic windfall of some $12 billion.[5] This radical reversal helped to jump-start Tehran's military rearmament—and to revive the Islamic Republic's regional ambitions.

Russia was responsible for the rest. By the year 2000, as part of its evolving entente with the Kremlin (detailed in the next chapter), Iran had become the third largest recipient of

Russian arms, with an estimated annual trade of $500 million.[6] Moscow's assistance went a long way toward resuscitating Tehran's strategic aspirations. In late 2000, buoyed by its expanding ties with the Kremlin, the Iranian government announced plans for a massive, twenty-five year national military modernization program—one entailing upgrades to its air defense, naval warfare, land combat capabilities and built almost entirely around Russian technology and weaponry.[7]

This sweeping agenda quickly took concrete form. In March 2001, Iranian President Mohammed Khatami headed a major defense delegation visit to Moscow, where he concluded a landmark arms and defense cooperation accord with Russian Defense Minister Sergei Ivanov. Under the agreement, the Kremlin pledged to supply the Islamic Republic with up to $7 billion worth of arms and defense materiel over the next few years, and to expand involvement in Iran's Bushehr nuclear reactor facility.[8] Among other things, the two countries agreed upon

- Tehran's receipt of aircraft munitions and parts for MiG-29 and Su-24MK fighter aircraft in use by the Iranian air force,
- A resumption of Russian assistance in constructing and outfitting shore-based installations for the Iranian navy's 877EKM-model submarines,
- An Iranian commitment to purchase and deploy Russian Antei-2500 anti-aircraft missile systems, and a pledge for future negotiations over additional units of the Tor-M1, Tor-M1T, and S-300 air defense systems from Russia's *Rosoboronexport* state arms agency, and
- Future military-technical cooperation, including deliveries of the S-300 PMU-1 and S-300 PMU-2 surface-to-air missile systems, radar stations, BMP-3 infantry fighting vehicles, modernized MiG-29 and Su-27 aircraft and missiles, naval landing craft, and patrol equipment.[9]

Fulfillment of this agreement alone was expected to be instrumental to Iran's military modernization plans.

Yet, less than seven months later, in early October 2001, Iranian Defense Minister Ali Shamkhani was lavishly received in Moscow by Russian Defense Minister Sergei Ivanov. The public four-day meeting yielded a far-reaching accord on security and arms (valued to be worth up to $2 billion).[10] During his talks with Ivanov, Shamkhani reportedly aired Tehran's requests for major upgrades for the army, navy, and air force, including Su-30 fighter aircraft, K-50 and K-52 attack and scout helicopters and state-of-the-art T-90 tanks.[11] Particular emphasis was placed on the purchase of air defense and battlefield missile systems, including Tochka-U and Iskander-E units, as well as the S-300 PMU advanced surface-to-air missile system.[12]

Russia's assistance was replicated, on a more modest scale, by China. Between 1993 and 1996, Chinese arms transfers to Iran stood at approximately $400 million. Between 1997 and 2000, that number had risen to $600 million.[13] The goods provided by the PRC included anti-ship cruise missiles, surface-to-air missiles, combat aircraft, and fast-attack patrol vessels, as well as advanced technology designed to expand the versatility of Iran's burgeoning cruise missile arsenal.[14] These weapons also became an important export commodity, with Iran providing Chinese-origin small arms to pro-Iranian insurgent groups attempting to spread its Revolution in places like Sudan, Lebanon, and Bosnia.[15]

In addition, China, along with North Korea, contributed significantly to what has become the central element of Iran's military rearmament—a revitalization of its naval forces. Tehran took delivery of Chinese naval missiles and patrol craft, as well as North Korean torpedo gunboats, in purchases that have boosted its ability to project power into the Strait of Hormuz and along key Persian Gulf shipping lanes.

The cumulative effects have been dramatic. Between 1996 and 2002, the Iranian military's stock of tanks and aircraft increased by approximately 30 percent. During the same period, Iran's arsenal of small arms grew by more than 64 percent.[16] Thus, even before the overthrow of Saddam Hussein's regime, Iran—with escalating assistance from Moscow, Beijing, and Pyongyang—was on track to become the dominant military power in the Persian Gulf. Even more significantly, it had grown to be capable of virtually controlling, albeit briefly, the flow of oil from the region,[17] gaining tremendous leverage, not just over its weaker Gulf neighbors, but over the U.S. and Europe as well.

The Iranian WMD Threat

Iran's rearmament did not stop there, however. As then–CIA Director George Tenet told Congress back in 1999, the Islamic Republic's "reformers and conservatives agree on at least one thing: weapons of mass destruction are a necessary component of defense and a high priority."[18] And, in tandem with its expanding conventional arsenal, Tehran emerged as the Persian Gulf's leading WMD power.

Ballistic missiles—Iran's efforts to develop a strategic offensive arsenal began during the Iran-Iraq War, in response to Iraq's devastating siege of Iranian cities.[19] They were reinforced by the 1991 Persian Gulf War, which showcased the importance of delivery systems like ballistic missiles to achieving strategic parity with the United States. According to the U.S. intelligence community's most recent assessment of global proliferation trends, "Iran's ballistic missile inventory is among the largest in the Middle East."[20] This arsenal includes several hundred *Scud-B* and *Scud-C* short-range ballistic missiles, mainly acquired from foreign suppliers like North Korea and China. Iran also has put a premium on indigenous missile development, and has managed to create production lines and accumulate notable quantities of a series of domestically developed short-range missiles, such as the *Zelzal*, *Samid*, and *Fateh*.[21]

The centerpiece of Iran's ballistic missile effort is the *Shahab-3*. In June 2003, the Islamic Republic successfully carried out what it termed to be the "final" test of the 1,300-kilometer-range missile, confirming its ability to target American allies like Israel and Turkey, as well as U.S. troops in the Persian Gulf. Since then, however, the *Shahab-3* has evolved significantly. In October 2004, in a speech before a forum on "Space and Stable National Security" at Tehran's Aerospace Research Institute, former Iranian President Ali Akbar Hashemi Rafsanjani announced that the Iranian regime has successfully increased the range of its premier missile to 2,000 kilometers (1,200 miles)—making it capable of targeting southeastern Europe.[22] At the same time, foreign estimates believe that Iran has succeeded in developing an indigenous missile infrastructure that would allow it to produce twenty or more of these missiles annually.[23]

For their part, opposition groups have charged that Iran's overt missile development masks a much larger clandestine endeavor—one that encompasses both the 4,000-kilometer (2,500 mile) range *Shahab-5* and even a follow-on intercontinental ballistic missile (ICBM) known as the "Kowsar."[24] This assessment rings true; according to U.S. intelligence officials, Iran is now estimated to have made sufficient headway to allow for the testing of ICBM components in 2005.[25]

Chemical weapons—Like its missile program, Tehran's efforts to acquire chemical weapons (CW) began during the Iran-Iraq War, when the Iranian leadership launched a national effort to develop a response to Iraqi chemical weapons attacks on Iranian troops. By 1992, the Islamic Republic had erected chemical weapons facilities in four separate regions of the country, and had commenced chemical weapons training for the *Pasdaran*.[26] Subsequently, during the mid-1990s, Iran's chemical weapons program received a substantial boost from foreign suppliers, such as China and North Korea, which provided the Iranian regime with critical precursor chemicals and key weapons know-how.[27]

Iran's Ballistic Missiles: Current and Projected Reach

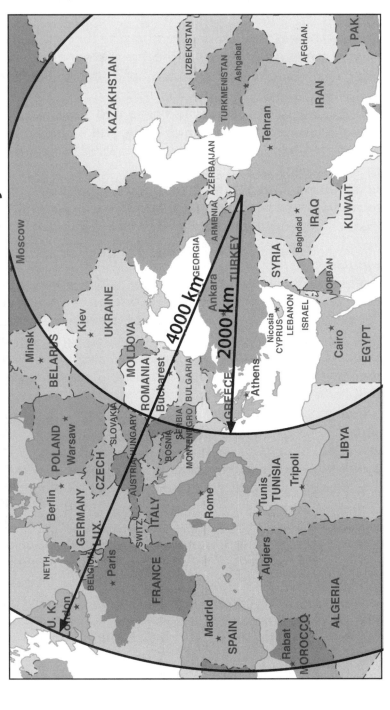

This effort paid off. By the mid-1990s, American estimates had begun to identify Iran as having the "most active" chemical weapons program in the developing world.[28] This was officially confirmed in September 2000, when the CIA told Congress that "Iran has a large and growing CW production capacity and already has produced a number of CW agents, including nerve, blister, choking, and blood agents . . . [and] a stockpile of at least several hundred metric tons of weaponized and bulk agent."[29]

Foreign governments have echoed this assessment. During a tour of Europe in the summer of 2002, the outgoing head of Israel's Mossad intelligence agency, Ephraim Halevy, warned Europeans about the expanding threat from Iran. Despite being a party to the 1993 Chemical Weapons Convention, Halevy stressed, Iran was in the process of constructing a "dual purpose civilian infrastructure which could be converted very speedily into production capabilities of large quantities of VX [nerve agent]."[30] And, by all indications, with Russian and Chinese assistance, Iran is forging ahead with plans for a self-sufficient chemical weapons development capability.

Biological weapons—By comparison, details about Iran's biological weapons (BW) effort are at best fragmentary. American officials believe that Tehran's BW program—which was also launched during the Iran-Iraq War—has now achieved a significant degree of maturity. Back in September 2000, testifying before the Senate on the topic of "Iran's Weapons of Mass Destruction," one top CIA nonproliferation official termed the Iranian biological weapons effort to be "in the late stages of development," and said Iran had already erected an indigenous BW "technical infrastructure."[31] This effort includes the ability to produce small quantities of biological agents, as well as having some capacity to weaponize it.

Proof of this progress was made public in May 2003, when the National Council of Resistance of Iran (NCRI) revealed new details about the Islamic Republic's biological weapons program. At a public briefing in Washington, representatives of the opposition group exposed Iran's efforts to develop plague and cholera, and its progress in weaponizing anthrax.[32] According to the NCRI, this effort is now expanding rapidly, and Iran's BW capability is expected to increase three-fold by the middle of 2005.[33]

Drifting toward Dominance

None of this was lost on Iran's neighbors. Some—like Libya and Syria—began to drift into Tehran's orbit. Until its abrupt about-face on WMD in mid-2003, the regime of Muammar Qaddafi was on track to become a major Iranian missile client, complete with technology-sharing arrangements and plans for co-production of Iranian missiles in Libya.[34] Damascus followed a similar path, relying heavily on Iranian assistance to facilitate the expansion of its strategic arsenal, and—more recently—to provide protection against the U.S. and Israel.[35]

Others were forced to seek an accommodation with Iran's ayatollahs. In 2000, Oman established a *modus vivendi* of sorts with the Islamic Republic through the codification of a sweeping agreement on military cooperation (albeit one that has since been denied by Muscat).[36] Officials in Kuwait subsequently followed suit, striking a similar bargain with Tehran in October 2002.[37] Even Saudi Arabia, previously a serious strategic competitor, came to terms with Iran in 2001 on a long-awaited agreement regarding security cooperation, narcotics interdiction, and terrorism—one effectively giving Iran a deciding voice in Saudi security policy. Explaining Riyadh's decision, Saudi Interior Minister Prince Nayef Bin Abdul Aziz hinted at a mature understanding of the new balance of power in the Gulf when he said that the House of Saud had embraced the idea of "Iran's security as our security."[38]

Thus, on the eve of the War on Terror, Iran had become, in the words of officials in Tehran, both a "regional power" and "a factor of stability in the region"—in other words, the natural center of gravity in the Persian Gulf.[39]

Crisis and Opportunity

For the Islamic Republic, poised on the brink of regional supremacy, the incursion of the U.S. into the Persian Gulf has posed an unprecedented challenge. And, in response, a momentous transformation has taken place in Iranian foreign policy.

The first glimmers of Iran's post-9/11 priorities became visible in late 2001, with the start of the U.S. campaign against the Taliban and al-Qaeda in Afghanistan. Publicly, Tehran opposed the idea of intervention, with Iranian leaders like Foreign Minister Kamal Kharrazi condemning a possible American incursion in no uncertain terms.[40] Privately, however, the Iranian leadership sang a rather different tune. After all, the Sunni Taliban's emergence in neighboring Afghanistan in the late 1990s had confronted the Shi'ite Islamic Republic with a serious ideological competitor for Muslim solidarity. As well, the Taliban quickly proved itself to be a bad neighbor following its ascension to power in Kabul in 1996, and Iran became forced to deal with incursions into its territory, as well as Afghanistan's transformation into a global source of opium—a fact that led to skyrocketing drug abuse and addiction rates within Iran.[41]

But cooperation quickly gave way to competition. The successful American ouster of the Taliban and al-Qaeda in late 2001—and the resulting political vacuum in Afghanistan—provided the Iranian regime with an unexpected opportunity to push east, and Iran's ayatollahs seized it.

Tehran's initial offensive was diplomatic. Iranian officials used the post-war turmoil in Afghanistan to spread the Islamic Republic's radical message and anti-American

Iranian Military Forces in Comparative Perspective

	IRAN	IRAQ	BAHRAIN	KUWAIT	OMAN	QATAR	SAUDI ARABIA	UNITED ARAB EMIRATES
Man-power	540,000	164,000 (combined soldier/police force)	11,200	15,500	41,700	12,400	124,500	50,500 (combined forces)
Ground combat	1,655 tanks 1,570 fighting vehicles 2,700 artillery	Inactive, to be reconstituted	140 tanks 277 fighting vehicles 48 artillery	293 tanks 530 fighting vehicles 100 artillery	107 tanks 225 fighting vehicles 148 artillery	30 tanks 260 fighting vehicles 56 artillery	795 tanks 4,500 fighting vehicles 410 artillery	441 tanks 1,250 fighting vehicles 399 artillery
Aerial warfare	209 combat aircraft 325 attack helicopters	Inactive, to be reconstituted	34 combat aircraft 39 attack helicopters	40 combat aircraft 23 attack helicopters	29 combat aircraft 41 attack helicopters	18 combat aircraft	360 combat aircraft 214 attack helicopters	54 combat aircraft 14 attack helicopters
Naval combat	6 submarines 29 combat vessels	Inactive, to be reconstituted	11 combat vessels	10 combat vessels	9 combat vessels	7 combat vessels	24 combat vessels	12 combat vessels
WMD programs and delivery systems	National nuclear program Biological weapons arsenal Chemical weapons arsenal Large ballistic missile arsenal containing SCUD-B and –C SRBMs, Shahab-3 MRBM, and suspected development of Shahab-4 extended-range MRBM and Shahab-5 ("Kosar") IRBM	No offensive chemical, biological, or nuclear capabilities discovered Small numbers of Al-Fateh, SCUB-B and Al-Samoud SRBMs unaccounted for; development work on MRBM capabilities found	No known chemical, biological, or nuclear capability No current ballistic missile capability	No known chemical, biological, or nuclear capability No current ballistic missile capability	No known chemical, biological, or nuclear capability No current ballistic missile capability	No known chemical, biological, or nuclear capability No current ballistic missile capability	No known chemical or biological capability Alleged nuclear contacts with Pakistan Small arsenal of CSS-2 MRBMs	No known chemical, biological or nuclear capability Rumored small arsenal of SCUD-B SRBMs

Sources: *The Military Balance 2003–2004* (London: Oxford University Press, 2003); *The Middle East Military Balance 2001–2002* (Boston: MIT Press, 2002); Anthony Cordesman, *Iran's Evolving Military Forces* (Washington: Center for Strategic and International Studies, July 2004); *World Ballistic Missile Capability Today* (Washington: George C. Marshall Institute, October 2004); Central Intelligence Agency website, November 2004; *Comprehensive Report of the Special Advisor to the Director of Central Intelligence on Iraq's WMD* (U.S. Central Intelligence Agency, September 30, 2004); *Washington Post*, September 26, 2004.

agenda via new radio broadcasting and media outlets, both in the former Soviet republic of Tajikistan and along the Iranian-Afghan border.[42] These channels provided Iran with the means to sow dissention between the U.S. and its local allies, and Tehran did just that, commencing propaganda efforts aimed at defaming and discrediting key Afghan political figures who were cooperating with the United States.[43]

Simultaneously, the Iranian regime wasted no time forging a special relationship with Ismail Khan, the governor of Afghanistan's western Herat province. Iranian assistance to Khan's militias—in the form of equipment, clothing, and even *Pasdaran* reinforcements—began as early as November 2001, and quickly engendered worries in Washington. So did reports that Iranian military officials were active in numerous Afghan provinces, where they were attempting to woo local chieftains away from cooperation with the emerging Afghan government.[44]

Iran did not stop there. Officials in Tehran threw their support behind Abdurashid Dostum, providing cash and military materiel to the notorious Afghan warlord.[45] These efforts were bolstered by an array of additional outreach in the form of "social programs" designed to win Afghan hearts and minds.[46]

The point of all of these efforts was clear. "Tehran is trying to create a sphere of influence in western Afghanistan and an area in which Tehran's remit exceeds that of Kabul," one American analyst commented in early 2002.[47]

Against this backdrop, Iran's ayatollahs were confronted with an even bigger challenge: the American-led invasion of Iraq. Iran's concern was not for its neighbor to the west; there was certainly no love lost between the two regional rivals. Not least, American preoccupation with "containing" Saddam, both during the 1990s and in the opening phases of the War on Terror, had been a boon to Iran, allowing it to rearm and to reestablish ties to countries in Europe and Asia.

But American successes in Afghanistan had already ensconced the pro-Western—though fragile—government of Hamid Karzai in Kabul, replacing the ideological threat of the Sunni Taliban with the more destabilizing prospect of a U.S. foothold on Iran's eastern border. The possibility of another regime change, this time in Baghdad, confronted Tehran with the possibility of a dangerous strategic encirclement, pinioned between two liberalizing, pro-American powers, and the frightening thought that Iraq's fall might just be a prelude to a similar American-driven transformation in their country.

As a result, Iran's chief international security policy-making organ, the Supreme National Security Council, convened a series of meetings in September 2002 to hammer out a new military strategy to deal with the looming threat of American military intervention in Iraq.[48] The resulting doctrine, dubbed "deterrent defense," was subsequently outlined in detail by Foreign Minister Kamal Kharrazi in a February 2003 interview with the conservative *Saisat e-Rouz* newspaper. According to Kharrazi, Tehran's new national security concept is designed to confront "a broad spectrum of threats to Iran's national security, among them foreign aggression, war, border incidents, espionage, sabotage, regional crises derived from the proliferation of WMD, state terrorism, and discrimination in manufacturing and storing WMD."[49] Left unspoken was the new doctrine's critical component, an embrace of "asymmetric warfare," ranging from terrorism to the use of WMD, as an answer to America's overwhelming military superiority.[50]

Ever since, Iran has been putting this policy into practice. It has done so on at least four fronts—by accelerating its pursuit of WMD, increasing its coalition-building efforts in the region, assuming a more aggressive regional military profile, and launching an unprecedented covert campaign aimed at perpetuating Iraq's instability.

Reinforcing WMD Alliances

Iran's deep ties to its WMD enablers, foremost among them Russia, China, and North Korea, did not end with the onset of the War on Terror. To the contrary, these connections have increased dramatically since September 2001, as Iran's ayatollahs have stepped up their WMD quest—and the Islamic Republic's suppliers have rallied to its side.

Russian president Vladimir Putin, for one, may have publicly broken with many in Moscow to support the U.S. in its campaign against al-Qaeda and the Taliban following the terrorist attacks on New York and Washington. Since then, however, worries over an extended American presence in Russia's Near Abroad of Central Asia and the Caucasus, together with economic priorities and the revival of old imperial impulses, have led the Kremlin to revert to Soviet type.[51]

Russian officials therefore have taken an increasingly defiant stance toward nuclear cooperation with Iran. In the summer of 2002, Russian First Deputy Foreign Minister Vyacheslav Trubnikov told Iranian officials during a state visit that "Russia does not accept President George W. Bush's view that Iran is part of 'an axis of evil.'"[52] And the Kremlin was quick to prove it; just weeks after the attacks on Washington and New York, Moscow had moved ahead with the Bushehr project, shipping a nuclear reactor shell for the massive facility over strenuous American objections.[53] That same summer, Russia's then–Prime Minister, Mikhail Kasyanov, traveled to Tehran to formalize a new agreement on atomic cooperation with the Islamic Republic. As part of that deal, Russia committed to building up to five additional reactors over the next ten years, both at Bushehr and in the western Iranian town of Ahvaz.[54] As of October 2004, Russia had announced the completion of the Bushehr reactor, and was moving toward the finalization of a nuclear fuel pact with Iran.[55]

At the same time, Russia has continued to provide critical assistance to Iran's ballistic missile programs. Persistent reports indicate that Russian entities have helped expand the range and sophistication of Iran's premier ballistic missile project, the *Shahab-3*.[56] These innovations were on display during Iran's August 2004 *Shahab* test, which showcased an extended-range variant with a reconfigured "baby bottle" nose cone—similar to those previously used on Soviet missiles.[57]

China has similarly ratcheted up its contacts with the Islamic Republic. Common concern over America's War on Terror led Iranian President Mohammed Khatami to undertake a landmark state visit to Beijing in June 2002. Khatami's visit, only the third ever made by any Iranian president, laid the groundwork for an expanded "strategic partnership" between the two countries. In addition to agreements on energy and expanded military-to-military contacts, Tehran successfully pressed for a deeper missile relationship with the PRC.[58] There can be little doubt regarding the organizing principle behind all of this cooperation. In the words of one conservative Iranian paper, "the strengthening of the Tehran-Beijing axis is of great importance" in the context of "confronting the unipolar world being considered by America."[59] Since then, an array of top Iranian officials, like Brigadier-General Mohammad Hejazi, Commander of the Islamic Republic's *Basij* militia, have traveled to Beijing to coordinate policies with the PRC on everything from border security to military planning.[60]

Likewise, North Korea's WMD ties to the Islamic Republic are hardly a thing of the past. In mid-2003, the two countries were reported to be in the advanced stages of negotiations regarding North Korean exports of its advanced *Taepo-Dong 2* intercontinental ballistic missile to Iran, as well as on a joint plan to produce nuclear warheads for those missiles.[61] Pyongyang's "Dear Leader," Kim Jong-Il, also continues to supply Tehran with numerous North Korean scientists and technical experts. According to an August 2003 report, "so many North Koreans are presently in Iran working on nuclear and ballistic missile projects, that a Caspian Sea resort has been furnished for their use."[62]

Coalition-Building, Iranian Style

For Iran's ayatollahs, American plans for a sea change in the region's political balance constitute a "serious threat to the security, independence, and stability of the Islamic countries."[63] They therefore hope that the creation of a regional security architecture of their own making will preclude a shift in the geopolitical status quo.

The first signs of this effort surfaced in May 2003, when Iran's envoy to the UN rekindled the notion of an Iranian-led regional bloc, akin to the one proposed by Tehran after the first Gulf War, in the pages of the *New York Times*. Iran, Ambassador M. Javad Zarif explained, "has a vested national security interest" in "stability and moderation in the region."[64] The idea subsequently was given new impetus in February 2004, when Iranian Foreign Minister Kamal Kharrazi used the occasion of the fourteenth International Persian Gulf conference in Tehran to position his government as an alternative to the U.S. in the Persian Gulf. "The regional states have unknowingly had a share in paying the price for the mistakes made by the Americans," Kharrazi emphasized. The answer, Iran's foreign minister said, was the creation of a regional coalition designed to preclude Western involvement.[65]

In turn, Tehran's coalition-building plans have found a receptive audience. Regional rogues, worried over the expansion of the U.S.-led War on Terror to target their own regimes, have embraced Iran's plans for the region. This was the case in early 2004, when Iran's Defense Minister, Rear Admiral Ali Shamkhani, embarked on a whirlwind tour of Syria and Lebanon. In Damascus, Shamkhani held a public summit with his Syrian counterpart, Lieutenant General Mustafa Tlas, at which the two hammered out a landmark "memorandum of understanding" paving the way for deeper defense-industrial cooperation between the two countries.[66] More significant still, the agreement formalized an unprecedented Iranian commitment to defend Syria in the event of either an Israeli or an American military offensive, formally placing the Ba'athist state under Iran's security umbrella.[67]

From Damascus, Shamkhani traveled to Beirut, where he held court with the upper echelons of the Lebanese government. In meetings with the country's President Emile Lahoud, as well as then–Prime Minister Rafiq Hariri, Parliamentary Speaker Nabih Berri, and Army Commander Michel Soleyman, Shamkhani pledged his government's commitment to closer military ties with Beirut—and an active Iranian role in Lebanon's nascent military modernization.[68]

The message of these meetings was unmistakable—the Israeli and American "enemy" would now "think a thousand times before attacking Lebanon."[69] For their part, officials in Beirut and Damascus have been quick to grasp the importance of the emerging "Tehran, Damascus, and Beirut axis" to the preservation of the region's old balance of power in the face of American encroachment.[70]

Even Egypt, a traditional adversary of Iran, has begun to come around. In December 2003, officials in Tehran initiated a historic reconciliation when Iranian President Mohammed Khatami met with his Egyptian counterpart, Hosni Mubarak, on the sidelines of the World Summit on Information Security in Geneva. The talks marked the first official meeting of its kind in over twenty years; shortly after Iran's 1979 Revolution, Egypt had provided refuge to deposed Iranian Shah Mohammed Reza Pahlavi in Cairo, leading to a breakdown in relations between the two countries. In their groundbreaking dialogue, the two leaders discussed regional security, Iraq, and closer political and strategic coordination.[71] The talks—and Iran's subsequent confidence-building measure of renaming a street honoring the assassin of the late Egyptian President Anwar Sadat—reflected a "new atmosphere" of "détente" between Iran and Egypt, in the words of Iranian officials.[72]

Moreover, Iran has managed to build bridges to its principal remaining regional rival, Turkey. A diplomatic rapprochement between Tehran and Ankara has been in the works since November 2002, when the Islamist Justice and Development Party (AKP) assumed power in Turkey. Since then, under the rubric of an "independent" foreign policy, Turkey has drifted toward alignment with Iran on an array of regional security and strategic issues. This newfound convergence was on display in July 2004, when Turkish Prime Minister Recep Tayyip Erdogan traveled to Tehran for a landmark summit with Iranian President Mohammed Khatami. The visit, the first such trip by a Turkish premier in eight years, yielded a series of accords on economic, political, and security issues, including the codification of an agreement to jointly combat both Kurdish rebels and Iranian insurgents.[73]

Even the Gulf Cooperation Council (GCC) has not proven immune to Iranian influence. Already worried over instability in post-war Iraq and increasingly threatened by Iran's military build-up, the six-member grouping has begun to toe Tehran's foreign policy line. By the summer of 2004, Iran had succeeded in codifying new agreements with four of its members—Saudi Arabia, Kuwait, Qatar, and Bahrain—over Gulf security.[74] Since then, in a recognition of Iran's growing regional clout, the GCC states have softened their tone toward Tehran, offering it—along with Iraq—greater participation in the regional bloc.[75]

A More Aggressive Military Posture

Over the past several years, massive defense acquisitions—courtesy of Russia, China, and North Korea—have steadily broadened Iran's strategic reach over vital Persian Gulf shipping lanes, to the point that Tehran now possesses the ability to interrupt oil supplies from the region.[76] The Islamic Republic, however, is not relying solely on foreign arms. During the Iran-Iraq War, Western embargos had left the Iranian regime vulnerable to Iraq's superior arsenal and firepower. Ever since, officials in Tehran have made major investments in military self-sufficiency a top priority.

The results are impressive; Iran is now capable of domestically producing a wide array of strategic weaponry, ranging from ballistic missiles to combat submarines.[77] Since 2003, the pace of this development has accelerated substantially, manifested in the public unveiling of a number of indigenously produced battlefield systems, including naval cruisers equipped with Iranian "Peykan" missile launchers (now in service in the Caspian Sea) and the "Sa'eqe" (Lightning), a domestically designed fighter jet intended to boost the country's "defensive power."[78] These efforts are seen by Iranian officials as essential to their country's continued regional status: "The production of modern weapons and the acquisition of new technology . . . are among the pillars of our national security," Mohsen Rezai, the influential former commander of the *Pasdaran*, has maintained publicly. "If Iran carefully implements the plan, it will be able to establish itself as the first regional power."[79]

In the shadow of Operation Iraqi Freedom, Iran has also put these capabilities on display through a series of far-reaching military maneuvers. Since mid-2002, these have included

- regional drills of armored detachments and infantry units of Iran's standing army, the *Artesh,* in central Iran;
- large-scale, multi-phase military maneuvers—complete with the deployment of ground troops and aerial combat units in "asymmetric warfare" exercises—by *Pasdaran* forces in central Iran;

- high-profile *Artesh* war games, involving conventional ground and aerial force deployments, intended to test the Iranian army's "speed, accuracy and mobility;"
- *Pasdaran* training drills aimed at "enhancing the country's military capabilities" near Iran's border with Afghanistan;
- naval drills designed to test coastal patrol and radar tracking capabilities, off Iran's Gulf and Caspian coasts;
- major *Pasdaran* maneuvers, complete with the deployment of some twenty thousand ground forces, near Iraq;
- multi-phase *Artesh* exercises, including both ground and aerial assault trainings, near Shiraz in Iran's southern province of Fars;
- large-scale maneuvers of ground forces in northwest Iran, near Azerbaijan;
- multiple submarine drills in the Persian Gulf, the Gulf of Oman, and parts of the Indian Ocean;
- large-scale *Pasdaran* ground force exercises in western Iran, designed to simulate an Iranian response to potential foreign invasion or attack; and
- Iran's largest ever military exercises, encompassing twelve army divisions, four air battalions and artillery detachments, in western and southern Iran.

Mirroring these efforts, Iran has begun to exhibit an increasingly aggressive profile in the Persian Gulf. Tehran is believed to have mounted short- and medium-range missiles aboard cargo vessels stationed in the Persian Gulf and the Strait of Hormuz—a move intended to increase the Islamic Republic's deterrence and force projection capabilities in the region.[80] And in June 2004, it fomented an international incident when it "confiscated" three British vessels and their crew of eight in the Shatt al-Arab waterway, accusing the ships of violating its territorial waters.[81] In the wake of the incident, a *Pasdaran* source publicly hinted that Tehran was using the detention to secure the release of Iranian operatives recently captured by Coalition troops in Iraq.[82] At least one analysis, however, provided a different motive: that the seizure was part of Iran's attempts to prevent Coalition allies from securing Iraqi ports—and to leave open the option for Iranian-sponsored strikes on Iraq's oil infrastructure aimed at destabilizing global markets.[83]

The Lebanonization of Iraq

In a July 2004 interview with London's *Daily Telegraph*, Iraq's new defense minister, Hazim al-Shaalan, provided a revealing look into the instability plaguing his country. "Iranian intrusion," he told the influential British daily, "has been vast and unprecedented since the establishment of the Iraqi state."[84]

Shaalan's comments are hardly an exaggeration. As U.S. plans for military action gathered steam in the spring of 2003, the Iranian regime authorized a massive military mobilization and formulated elaborate plans for the infiltration of its western neighbor, complete with orders for *Pasdaran* units to take control of key Iraqi population centers and expand contacts with sympathetic Iraq-based groups.[85] Tehran was thus positioned to take advantage of the political vacuum that emerged after Saddam Hussein's overthrow. Since the official end of major combat operations in Iraq in May 2003, Iran has launched a massive strategic offensive designed to destabilize the post-totalitarian political system there. This effort encompasses

- *The infiltration of hundreds of intelligence agents and Pasdaran operatives into post-war Iraq.* According to U.S. intelligence reports, Iranian agents have been tasked with uncovering details of U.S. military planning, and of enlisting Iraqis to carry out attacks against Coalition forces and Western interests within the country.[86] To support them, Iran has established an extensive network of safe-houses and institutional mechanisms to facilitate Iranian intelligence and covert operations on Iraqi territory.[87] In a summer

75

2004 meeting with his Jordanian counterpart, Iraqi Interior Minister Falah Hassan al-Naqib publicly acknowledged this involvement when he stressed Iran's direct role in "the terrorist and sabotage operations being carried out in Iraq."[88]

- *The relaxation of border controls to permit the infiltration of organized criminal elements and terrorists into Iraq.* As a result, Iranian drug smuggling networks have established a major foothold within Iraq, using religious tourism and trade as a cover for their activities.[89] Persistent reports from allied factions within Iraq suggest that Iran continues to allow Islamic militants from groups like the al-Qaeda-affiliated *Ansar al-Islam* to traverse Iranian territory into Iraq, and to reinforce their compatriots with new weapons.[90] In fact, *Pasdaran* officials themselves have admitted that Iran continues to allow master terrorist Abu Musab al-Zarqawi to traverse its territory with impunity.[91]

- *The elimination of independent Iraqi religious leaders that could pose a challenge to Iran's religious primacy. Pasdaran* operatives, for example, are believed to be responsible for the summer 2003 assassination in Najaf of the Ayatollah Muhammad Bakr al-Hakim, the independent-minded head of the Supreme Council for the Islamic Revolution in Iraq (SCIRI).[92] Other Iraqi religious leaders, like the Ayatollah Abdel Majid al-Khoei, similarly have been murdered by pro-Iranian forces.[93]

- *Bankrolling organized anti-Coalition militias now active within Iraq.* Most prominently, Iran is known to have provided major funding to firebrand Shi'ite cleric Moqtada al-Sadr's *Al-Mahdi* Army—enabling the radical militia to continue to menace Coalition military forces.[94] Additional financial support from Tehran has also gone to the SCIRI's semi-autonomous armed militia, the *Badr* Organization.[95] Iran is even said to have allocated some $45 million to arm the military wings of Iraqi political parties.[96]

- *Financing a large-scale media outreach designed to win Iraqi hearts and minds.* Directed in large part by the *Pasdaran*, Iran's efforts far outstrip the public diplomacy being undertaken by the U.S. and its Coalition allies in the former Ba'athist state. As of November 2003, the U.S.-led Coalition controlled one operational television station, two radio channels, and one newspaper—compared with over forty Iranian-supported or directed broadcast media outlets.[97]

- *The recruitment of Iraqi Shi'ite cadres to foment political unrest at Iran's direction.* These activities include the formation of a cadre of radicalized Iraqi youth to be mobilized against the country's nascent democratic processes.[98] Moreover, Iran is providing substantial incentives for enlistment; according to one CIA report, Iran has offered "a bounty on U.S. forces of U.S. $2,000 for each helicopter shot down, $1,000 for each tank destroyed, and $500 for each U.S. military personnel killed."[99] Much of this recruitment is believed to be accomplished by providing bribes and pay-offs to Shi'ite clerics in Iraq in exchange for promoting Iran's radical message.[100]

- *Providing arms and training to Iraqi insurgents.* Regular arms shipments from Iran have reportedly provided anti-Coalition irregulars with an array of weaponry, ranging from small arms to heavy artillery.[101] Iran's *Pasdaran* has even gone as far as establishing training camps on the Iran-Iraq border and teaching guerrilla warfare, explosives, and military techniques to hundreds of young Iraqi radicals.[102]

- *Mobilizing its terrorist surrogates to exploit the political vacuum of post-Saddam Iraq.* With Iran's blessing, Hezbollah and Hamas have established an extensive presence on the territory of the former Ba'athist regime, with offices in urban centers like Nasariah, Basra, and Safwan, and are recruiting Iraqi teenagers and young adults to their ranks.[103] In particular, Hezbollah's infiltration has been so successful that the Lebanese Shi'ite militia is said to have assumed police duties in some Iraqi cities.[104]

- *The promotion of religious and sectarian strife among Iraq's disparate religious and national minorities.* Most directly, Iran has provided political and financial backing to Iraq's Turkoman Shi'ites in their struggle against the country's powerful Kurdish minority and supported Kurdish groups (such as the Patriotic Union of Kurdistan, headed by Jalal Talibani) in their efforts to establish an autonomous state.[105] By February 2004, these activities had become so alarming that members of Iraq's Governing Council warned publicly that "some neighboring countries" were encouraging "sectarian sedition" in the country.[106]

Such a campaign does not come cheap, and Iran has marshaled extensive financial resources in support of its activities in Iraq. In an April 2004 interview with *Al-Sharq al-Awsat*, one Iranian defector claimed that Iran already had spent some $1 billion on the Iraqi insurgency, and was continuing to spend more than $70 million per month on activities in Iraq.[107] According to U.S. and Israeli intelligence sources, the sum provided by Iran to Moqtada al-Sadr's radical *Al-Mahdi* army alone is believed to be as much as $80 million.[108]

What drives these efforts? It is certainly not the desire to create a true Islamic Republic of Iraq. Officials in Tehran understand full well that Iraq's holy cities, Najaf and Karbala, supercede Iranian religious sites in the theological hierarchy of Shi'a Islam, and that the emergence of an Iraqi theocracy might well relegate Iran to the role of a satellite, at least in religious terms. Rather, the goals of Iran's ayatollahs are more strategic—and more ambitious. They realize that success in Iraq is central to the long-term realization of American strategy in the Middle East. And they hope that a U.S. failure will blunt the impact of Iraq's liberation on their own restive population, and derail Washington's plans for a sweeping post-totalitarian transition in the region. In the words of Yahya Rahim Safavi, commander of Iran's *Pasdaran*: "If [American] strategy fails heavily in Iraq, it will undoubtedly stop. Otherwise it may extend to neighboring countries."[109]

Trouble Ahead

These elaborate maneuvers underscore an unmistakable reality: Iran today constitutes the preeminent military power in the Persian Gulf, and the region's dominant political and strategic force. And, fueled by the political instability of the War on Terror, Tehran's economic fortunes—and its geopolitical aspirations—are expanding.

After all, Iran is a regional energy superpower in its own right. Home to 10 percent or more of the world's oil, it is the second largest exporter in the Organization of Petroleum Exporting Countries (OPEC), producing an average of 3.9 million barrels of oil per day.[110] Iran also sits atop the world's second-largest natural gas reserves, estimated at some 940 trillion cubic feet (second only to Russia).[111] And, over the past several years, a series of major oil finds—including the Azadegan field and Bangestan reservoirs in southern Iran and the offshore Dasht-e-Abadan site near the southwestern port city of Abadan—have substantially boosted the country's projected oil reserves.[112]

These discoveries, coupled with the rising price of crude oil, have done more than simply give Tehran a growing foothold in the world energy market; they have positioned the Iranian regime as a major strategic asset for energy-hungry states. Already, China's burgeoning domestic crude oil demand has led officials in Beijing to embrace an energy alliance with Iran's ayatollahs. In 2004 alone, the two countries signed two massive accords, estimated to be worth some $100 billion over the next twenty-five years, granting Chinese firms the rights to develop Iranian oil and natural gas reserves.[113] The resulting strategic partnership increasingly threatens to undermine the international consensus surrounding the need to contain Iran's nuclear program, and weakens the effectiveness of any economic sanctions attempted by the international community.

Even more ominously, Iran's capacity for troublemaking is poised to grow dramatically. According to U.S. government estimates, the Islamic Republic's official budget of $127 billion for 2004–2005, approximately half of which is tied to oil earnings, is based on revenue projections of the price of crude oil at $19.90 per barrel.[114] The dramatic rise in oil prices since the start of the War on Terror, therefore, has substantially expanded Iran's coffers. Even by conservative estimates, Tehran is expected to reap upwards of $30 billion in extra revenues for every year oil prices remain in the mid-$40 a barrel range—dramatically increasing the funds available to the Iranian regime for defense procurement and WMD development, not to mention insurgency operations in Iraq and support for terrorist groups abroad.

CHAPTER 4

The Northern Front

Iran's public successes in the Persian Gulf have been matched, more quietly, in another arena. Ever since the collapse of the Soviet Union, officials in Tehran have eyed the fledgling republics of Central Asia and the Caucasus hungrily, seeing in those states an opportunity for expanded regional influence, and for new outposts for their Islamic Revolution. For most of the past decade, however, they have steered clear of both regions as part of a tacit understanding with Russia.

All of that is now changing. Policy makers in Moscow, worried over the entrenchment of a lasting American strategic presence in their backyard, have relaxed their historic opposition to Tehran's meddling. In response, Iran's ayatollahs have opened up a new front against the U.S. in Central Asia and the Caucasus.

In the energy-rich Caspian Basin, Iran has adopted a new, more aggressive military profile, one aimed at confronting what officials in Tehran call a "foreign irritant"—the United States.[1] Tehran is also stepping up its efforts to create a regional coalition capable of countering American influence, and expanding its claim on energy exports from the Caspian Sea. Iran has even ratcheted up its relationship with Turkey, developing major economic, political, and security ties with one of the United States' most vital regional allies.

New Frontiers for the Revolution

Although it is being put into practice against the backdrop of the War on Terror, Iran's strategy in the "post-Soviet space" is hardly new. Its roots stretch back more than a decade, to the collapse of the Soviet Union in 1991.

Before that time, Iran's historic backyard was largely off-limits to the Islamic Republic, both as a matter of policy and of practice. During the nineteenth century, Iran's presence in the Caucasus—the legacy of conquests under the Persian Empire—had been progressively whittled away by a series of conflicts with Tsarist Russia. In 1813, under the Treaty of Gulistan, Iran lost the territory of contemporary Azerbaijan, as well as the portions of Georgia then under its control.[2] Fifteen years later, as part of the Treaty of Turkmenchai, Iran ceded part of modern-day Armenia, as well as the enclave of Nakhichivan.[3] With the emergence of the Soviet Union in 1918, any lingering influence wielded by Tehran evaporated, and Iran's Caucasus policy took a back seat to good relations with Moscow for the next seventy years.

With the implosion of the Soviet sphere, however, all that began to change. Moscow's misfortune was Tehran's gain; the break-up of the Soviet bloc spawned eight new states in Central Asia and the Caucasus, most of them majority-Muslim, and several with historic ties to Tehran. For Iran's ayatollahs, who had been looking north since the 1979 Islamic Revolution, this opening revived aspirations of a regional Islamic coalition—a massive Muslim bloc of some one hundred million souls to replace the U.S.S.R., with Iran at its helm.[4] It also prompted the implementation of a far-reaching strategy designed to win hearts and minds in the former Soviet republics.

The reasons for Iran's interest were obvious. During the Cold War, the Soviet republics were publicly staunchly secular, taking their cues from the Kremlin. Their emergence as independent states thus heralded a religious revival—one that the Islamic Republic was well positioned to exploit. The collapse of the Soviet Union created a "great market for the introduction of Islam," and imposed a "religious duty" on Iran to spread its radical message, Iranian officials intoned at the time.[5] It was a mission made all the more pressing by the possibility of an upsurge in Western influence or, worse yet, "American morals," among these countries.[6] Tehran, therefore, allocated hundreds of millions of dollars—and massive diplomatic resources—for a regional foothold intended to spread the Islamic Revolution.[7]

Iran's influence soon became apparent. In Tajikistan, the region's only other Farsi-speaking state, Iran fostered a radicalization of Islamist opposition factions, as well as facilitating the emergence of revolutionary committees based on the Iranian model, right down to their anti-American ideology.[8] Iran's encouragement, and its cultural outreach—manifested through Tehran's support of Persian language in Tajik schools—found fertile soil in Dushanbe, where officials extolled the idea that historically Iran and Tajikistan had lived "in a single state."[9] By 1994, these inroads had become so substantial that senior U.S. officials were publicly warning of Iran's support of terrorism in the fragile former Soviet republic.[10] (Iran's successes also encouraged Washington to adopt a *laissez faire* attitude toward the Kremlin's decision to pursue a political and military retrenchment in Tajikistan.[11])

Iran's religious appeal was matched on the economic front. Officials in Tehran wasted no time in resuscitating the moribund Economic Cooperation Organization (ECO)—originally founded in 1985 by Iran, Turkey, and Pakistan—expanding the group's membership to include the new states of the Caucasus and Central Asia and mapping out an ambitious agenda for regional economic integration. The aim of this construct was simple: strategic influence. As then-President Rafsanjani explained to reporters on the eve of the ECO's February 1992 summit in Tehran: "[t]he ECO members as well as the Persian Gulf littoral states can form a powerful political-economic body in the region and present themselves as a world power."[12]

The Islamic Republic's economic jockeying did not stop there. Iran strengthened its bilateral ties to Azerbaijan, signing a series of commercial deals in the summer of 1991 and subsequently inking agreements for "cultural" exchanges between the two countries, laying the groundwork for Tehran's increased influence in the Caucasus state.[13] Iranian leaders like Foreign Minister Ali Akbar Velayati also embarked on regional missions aimed at forging new commercial links with Kazakhstan, Kyrgyzstan, and Turkmenistan.[14]

Fresh from its military defeat at the hands of Saddam Hussein's regime, Tehran also saw the Soviet collapse as an important opportunity to secure new military suppliers. Armenia's robust defense-industrial infrastructure, inherited from the Soviet Union, made it a particularly attractive source for high-tech arms, and Iranian officials quickly reached out to the newly independent Caucasus state for military supplies.[15] In return for arms assistance, the Iranian regime actively backed Armenia in its post–Cold War clash with neighbor and rival Azerbaijan over the disputed Nagorno-Karabagh region. By the middle of 1992, Iran had already begun playing a destabilizing role in the conflict, signing energy deals with Yerevan that broadened and perpetuated its war effort against Azerbaijan.[16]

At the same time, Iran was working actively in another arena. The collapse of the Soviet bloc had led to a corresponding decline in the once ironclad safeguards surrounding the U.S.S.R.'s massive nuclear arsenal. This was a development that was not lost on officials in Tehran, who launched a series of efforts aimed at acquiring nuclear warheads and fissile material from several former Soviet states.[17]

Iranian officials made no secret of the goals behind this outreach: the creation of a massive regional coalition of Islamic states, bound together economically, politically, and culturally, and armed with nuclear weapons. The Soviet

Union, Iran's ayatollahs believed, could be replaced, at least in part, by a "Union of Islamic Republics."[18]

Strange Bedfellows

Over time, however, these overtures took a back seat to another, even more promising enterprise—strategic partnership with Russia.

The collapse of the Soviet Union had unleashed a wave of ethnic and religious separatism in Russia's turbulent "Southern Rim" of Central Asia and the Caucasus. Kremlin officials watched this development with deep apprehension, afraid that the emerging extremism could spill over into parts of the Russian Federation. Having seen Iran's domination of Lebanon in the early 1980s, and its global efforts to "export the revolution" thereafter, they also became justifiably worried about Tehran assuming a similar role on their periphery. The Iranian regime, meanwhile, was still struggling to reconstitute its regional standing and its military might in the aftermath of its costly eight-year war with Iraq. The result was a marriage of convenience that included Russian sales of commercial arms (and later nuclear know-how) to Iran in exchange for a quiet understanding that Tehran would steer clear of meddling in the newly independent states of Russia's Near Abroad.

Russia's primary motivations were strategic, but practical reasons for cooperation also existed. Russia's defense industry had not weathered the post-Soviet transition well, and Iran promised to be a significant source of income for the battered Russian armaments sector. One leading expert would later admit that Russia "should be grateful to Iran for having provided tens of thousands of Russian companies with 70 percent of their work."[19]

The Russo-Iranian entente may have started as a marriage of convenience, but by the late 1990s, it had become much more. In January of 1996, President Boris Yeltsin replaced his docile, Western-leaning foreign minister, Andrei Kozyrev, with Yevgeny Primakov, the wily spymaster who headed Russia's foreign intelligence agency, the *Sluzhba Vneshnei Rozvedki*, or SVR. The reshuffle marked the start of a new era in Russia's Middle East policy. In his day, Primakov had served as the chief Middle East specialist for the government of Leonid Brezhnev, and been the Kremlin's *de facto* point-man on ties with Iraq, Libya, and the PLO during the 1970s and 1980s.[20] Primakov's ascendance, therefore, repositioned Moscow as a geopolitical counterweight to Washington in the Middle East.

Moscow's attitudes toward Tehran underwent a corresponding change. Under Kozyrev, Russia had aligned itself with the U.S. in opposing Iran. This was not without good reason; at least some policy makers in Moscow saw Iran's potential to export fundamentalism to Russia's periphery as the cardinal threat facing the Kremlin in the post–Cold War era.[21] Under Primakov, however, these worries gave way to a more benign view of the Islamic Republic. Ties with Tehran became seen in Moscow as a pivotal geopolitical alliance, and an important hedge against perceived American hegemony in the Middle East.

The strategic partnership nurtured under Primakov took on a new dimension with Vladimir Putin's assumption of the Russian presidency in the last days of 1999. Far from breaking with his predecessor's embrace of the ayatollahs, Putin strengthened the Kremlin's tilt toward Tehran. In November 2000, in a public show of support for the Iranian regime, Russia officially abrogated the 1995 Gore-Chernomyrdin Agreement, under which Moscow had agreed to curtail new nuclear-related exports to the Islamic Republic. The importance of ties with the Islamic Republic also became a feature of the foreign policy blueprint issued by the Russian Foreign Ministry the same year.[22]

Tehran, in turn, became an active broker of the Kremlin's ambitious regional agenda in the "post-Soviet space," agitating for a Russia-led grouping intended to counter American influence in the region. In late 1999, Iranian Foreign Minister Kamal Kharrazi himself floated the issue of enhanced bilateral relations between Iran and Armenia in the context of such a Russia-led bloc.[23] Over time, Iran's negotiations with Turkmenistan and Armenia also yielded a convergence of policies regarding Caspian energy issues and regional security, greatly strengthening Russia's position in the region.[24]

By the latter part of 2001, as a result of these steps, the strategic ties between Moscow and Tehran had grown into a vibrant security relationship—one increasingly threatening to American interests in Central Asia and the Caucasus.

America's Intrusion

September 11, 2001, irrevocably shattered this post–Cold War strategic balance. In the aftermath of the 9/11 attacks, the U.S. commenced an unprecedented strategic expansion into the "post-Soviet space" as part of its campaign against the Taliban and al-Qaeda in Afghanistan. Over the next year, through its diplomatic overtures to the countries of the Caucasus and Central Asia, the White House succeeded in codifying agreements for military basing with Uzbekistan and Kyrgyzstan, hammering out a deal with Kazakhstan establishing overflight rights and permission for materiel transshipment in support of American military operations, and acquiring contingency use of Tajikistan's national airport in Dushanbe.[25] As part of these contacts, the Bush administration also dramatically deepened economic assistance to the region (nearly tripling its aid to Uzbekistan alone between October 2001 and September 2002).[26] By mid-2003, Washington had established "forward" bases, housing a combined total of close to three thousand troops, in Uzbekistan and Kyrgyzstan, and developed deep tactical and intelligence cooperation with four out of five of the Central Asian states.[27]

Since then, the Pentagon's strategic priorities have strengthened this regional focus. For much of the preceding decade, the Soviet Union's collapse had by and large not been reflected in the strategic posture of the United States. Instead, American military planners chose simply to substitute the Russian Federation for the U.S.S.R. as its principal adversary.[28] All of that is now changing. The Bush administration, recognizing the fundamental changes that have taken place in the pace, scope, and nature of threats confronting the U.S., has embarked upon a massive force transformation—one designed to make the U.S. military capable of achieving assurance, dissuasion, deterrence, and defense against any potential adversary in any environment.[29]

The "post-Soviet space" has become a key arena for these efforts. American officials have identified a "broad arc of instability" stretching from the Middle East into Northeast Asia.[30] And they have commenced a global realignment of U.S. forces in order to gain strategic control of those theaters.[31]

These developments have been watched with growing alarm, both in Moscow and in Tehran. Initially, Washington's plans had met with the blessing of Russian President Vladimir Putin. The steady expansion of America's presence, however, has fanned Russian fears of a long-term U.S. foothold, and a corresponding diminution of Moscow's influence in its geopolitical backyard. Iran's ayatollahs have similar worries. When coupled with American advances in Iraq and Afghanistan, the Iranian regime now faces the very real threat of encirclement by the U.S. and its Coalition of the Willing.

In response, Iran has launched—and the Kremlin appears to have endorsed—a multifaceted strategic offensive aimed at rolling back America's recent advances, and reestablishing Iran as a dominant regional player.

An Anti-American Axis

In April 2003, with active military operations underway in neighboring Iraq, Iran quietly dispatched a diplomatic delegation to the Caucasus. Over the course of three days, the high-level group, headed by Foreign Minister Kharrazi, visited the republics of Azerbaijan, Georgia, and Armenia, meeting with top government officials and heads of state. To each, Kharrazi and his companions delivered the same proposal—the creation of a common regional security framework for Georgia, Armenia, Azerbaijan, Russia, Iran, and Turkey as an alternative to cooperation with "external forces."[32]

Kharrazi's proposal was certainly not Tehran's first effort at regional coalition building; Iran's ayatollahs had been attempting to exclude a Western strategic presence from the Caucasus and Central Asia for years. But these efforts have intensified dramatically since the start of the War on Terror.

With Armenia, its principal ally in the Caucasus, Tehran is moving toward closer strategic ties on an array of issues, ranging from counterterrorism to military exchanges, in an effort to derail closer ties between Armenia and the United States.[33] These links were on display during Iranian Defense Minister Ali Shamkhani's March 2002 trip to Yerevan, which yielded a Memorandum of Understanding between Shamkhani and his Armenian counterpart, Serzh Sarkisyan, on a broad range of "bilateral military cooperation," including arms trade.[34] Subsequently, in September 2004, Iranian President Mohammed Khatami himself reaffirmed these bonds when he traveled to Armenia as part of a three-country tour designed to deepen Iran's ties to the Caucasus.[35] It's no wonder that top Armenian officials now view the Islamic Republic as a "guarantor of stability" in the Caucasus.[36]

A similar effort is underway in Turkmenistan, where the Iranian regime has assumed a leading role in assisting the former Soviet republic's military armament. In October 2003, Iran's Defense Minister, Ali Shamkhani, approved the long-term loan of seven coastal patrol vessels and one destroyer to the government of President Saparmurat Niyazov under preferential conditions and at a considerable discount.[37] Since then, Iranian officials and their Turkmen counterparts have forged additional accords on cooperation in "security matters" ranging from counterterrorism to mutual defense.[38]

Tehran has also taken a series of steps to coordinate regional policies with its chief strategic partner, Russia. At the outset of the U.S.-led campaign in Afghanistan, Moscow and Tehran began discussions of a common political and security agenda for Central Asia and the Caucasus—one designed to forestall the creation of a U.S.-backed government in Kabul.[39] Since then, the two countries have made substantial progress, animated by mutual fears over the growing American strategic presence in Central Asia and the Caucasus. And officials in Tehran have stressed the need for greater "cooperation" and "integration" among regional nations in response to America's inroads—with the relationship between Moscow and Tehran serving as the principal driver.[40]

Russian officials, for their part, have taken pains to support Iran's chief strategic priority: its atomic drive. In October 2004, Russian Foreign Minister Sergei Lavrov paid a high-profile visit to Tehran, where he met with his counterpart, Kamal Kharrazi, and with Hassan Rowhani, the Secretary of Iran's Supreme National Security Council. The meetings yielded mutual affirmations of the strong strategic bonds between Russia and Iran, and an important symbolic message from the Kremlin—support of Iran's inalienable right to nuclear technology.[41] Since then, Russian dignitaries like Federal Atomic Agency Director Alexandr Rumyantsev and Federation Council Chairman Sergei Mironov have visited Tehran to confirm their country's commitment to ongoing atomic cooperation, and to a coordinated approach toward "peace and security" in the Middle East.[42]

Iranian leaders have made no secret of the goals behind these maneuvers. According to officials like Brigadier General Yahya Rahim-Safavi, the commander of Iran's

Pasdaran, foreign powers have "strategic plans to get their hands on the energy, oil, gas, and other resources" of the Caspian, as well as the Persian Gulf.[43] Tehran's remedy for the problem is a regional coalition designed to exclude foreign influence in Central Asia and the Caucasus.

Iran's "Great Game"

Iran is also making progress on another front. Ever since the emergence of Azerbaijan, Kazakhstan, and Turkmenistan as independent states in 1991—and the subsequent discovery of major energy deposits within their borders—the Caspian Basin has been the site of a mounting struggle for economic, military, and strategic influence by an array of global players.[44]

Over the years, Iran has played a central role in this competition, and for good reason. During the Cold War, Tehran had to contend with only one regional actor in the Caspian, the Soviet Union. And, as a result of treaties signed with Moscow, the Islamic Republic staked a claim to virtually half of the Caspian.[45] But with the Soviet collapse and the emergence of a new, five-state Caspian order, Iran's stake was reduced to a small slice of Caspian coastline and comparatively small offshore deposits. Moreover, Iran's ayatollahs were suddenly faced with the specter of Western involvement, which threatened to transform the Caspian into another Persian Gulf and cause Tehran to lose its foothold there.

This contest has now entered a new phase. Today, Tehran is increasing its efforts to gain critical mass in the volatile Caspian energy market, and to undermine the emergence of pro-Western energy routes, such as the Baku-Tbilisi-Ceyhan (BTC) pipeline,[46] which have the potential to sideline Iran in the regional energy picture.

With Yerevan, Iran has successfully negotiated a massive energy accord, effectively making Armenia a major client state of the Islamic Republic. The deal, concluded in May

2004, entails the construction of a bilateral natural gas pipeline linking the two nations, and large-scale Iranian gas deliveries (eventually as much as forty-seven billion cubic meters per year) beginning in early 2007.[47]

This energy partnership has attracted regional attention. Since Georgia's "Rose Revolution" in late 2003, the country's new president, Mikheil Saakashvili, has shown a keen interest in expanding relations with Iran.[48] Officials in Tbilisi thus have drawn closer to Tehran on energy issues, expressing their interest in importing Iranian gas, and in linking the former Soviet republic to the emerging Iran-Armenia pipeline route as a means of moving energy through the Caucasus.[49]

Iran has also made progress with Tajikistan. In September 2004, as part of a high-profile diplomatic tour of three former Soviet republics, Iranian President Mohammed Khatami visited Tajikistan and came to terms with officials in Dushanbe on expanding the already vibrant strategic ties between the two countries with the completion of a hydropower station—one that would eliminate Tajikistan's current energy deficit and provide enough of a surplus to export energy to both Iran and Russia.[50]

At the same time, Tehran is actively pushing for deeper energy integration with Kazakhstan. Kazakhstan currently exports more than eighteen million barrels of oil a year to Iran as part of an "oil swap" agreement hammered out with the Islamic Republic in 2000, under which Kazakh oil is shipped from Iranian ports on the Caspian Sea for domestic consumption, while oil from southern Iran is exported from Iranian ports on the Persian Gulf and sold on the world market. The Islamic Republic is working to expand this arrangement, and has upgraded and increased the capacity of its Caspian ports in hopes of "doubling" the volume of Kazakh oil swaps in the near future.[51]

Iran's greatest energy inroads, however, have been with Russia. Since 2002, Moscow and Tehran have taken a series of steps to coordinate energy policies.[52] The two countries, which have been at odds in the past over the legal delimitation of the Caspian Sea, have gravitated toward consensus regarding regional security—and the prevention of foreign intrusion into the energy-rich area.[53] They have also begun discussions regarding a regional energy cartel: a Kremlin-led natural gas union modeled after OPEC. "The Russian government is coordinating its policies on the gas market with Iran," Alexandr Maryasov, the Russian ambassador to Tehran, told the *Tehran Times* newspaper in mid-2004. "To this effect, Iranian Ministry of Oil and the Russian Ministry of Energy have set up working groups... The two countries hold the largest gas reserves in the world and they should cooperate and not compete."[54]

Caspian Militarization

In support of these efforts, Iran has adopted a more aggressive strategic profile in the Caspian. In the spring of 2001, General Mohammed Salimi, the commander of the Iranian armed forces, publicly warned that the Islamic Republic stood ready to respond militarily to Western interference in Caspian affairs.[55] Subsequently, in a blatant display of gunboat diplomacy, Iran menaced neighboring Azerbaijan over disputed energy sources,[56] leading to the effective—albeit temporary—pullout of several Western multinational oil companies from the region.

Since then, Iran has increased its potential for trouble-making. Already boasting the second largest fleet in the Caspian (after Russia), Iran's naval assets have grown substantially in the last several years. According to Western intelligence estimates, Iran now bases about one-third of its entire navy—some sixty-five ships, including eight surface combat vessels, one submarine, and fifty-six small patrol boats—in the Caspian.[57] Tehran, however, hopes to expand this Caspian contingent still further. In April 2004, Iranian Naval Commander Rear Admiral Abbas Mohtaj announced his country's plans for a new naval squadron for the region, complete with warships, supply craft, Russian-made *Kilo*-class submarines, mini-subs, and additional marine detachments.[58] Even more ominously, Western officials believe that Iran is now working on a new basing mode for its ballistic missile arsenal, and will soon deploy a range of short- and medium-range missiles aboard cargo vessels stationed in the Caspian.[59]

Needless to say, a force of this magnitude—controlled by Iran's unpredictable ayatollahs—could pose a grave threat to regional security in Central Asia and the Caucasus, and to the stability of energy exports from one of the world's most important energy producing regions.

Squeezing Azerbaijan

In tandem with these high-profile regional maneuvers, the Iranian regime has also embarked upon a more clandestine endeavor—a concerted campaign aimed at destabilizing the pro-Western Aliyev regime in Azerbaijan.

Such activities are not entirely without precedent. After all, Azerbaijan poses a major strategic challenge for Iran. In 1813, as a result of the Treaty of Gulistan, Iran lost most of the area of modern Azerbaijan to the Russians.[60] The southern regions of the Azeri homeland, where many Azeris live today, however, remained under Iranian control. The demographic impact of this historical decision was profound: Azeris today compose between a quarter and a third of the total Iranian population (between sixteen and twenty million)—more than twice the total population of the Republic of Azerbaijan.[61]

Understandably, the specter of Azeri separatism has haunted Tehran ever since the Soviet collapse. Simply put, the Iranian leadership believes that a politically vibrant and economically prosperous Azerbaijan will feed latent separatist tendencies among Iran's own Azeri population—with potentially disastrous consequences for the Islamic Republic. Over the years, therefore, Iran's ayatollahs have attempted to curtail this possibility through both practical measures (such as a 1993 ban on intermarriage between Iranian Azeris and Azerbaijani Azeris) and appeals to the Islamic unity of the region.[62] More ominously, Iran has undertaken an orchestrated campaign of "Islamization" along both sides of its border with Azerbaijan, sponsoring the operations of existing Shi'ite mosques and *madrassas* (religious schools) and the creation of new ones.[63]

Tehran's worries have been brought into sharp focus since the start of the U.S.-led War on Terror, and Azerbaijan's assumption of a leading role in it.[64] In response, Iran has taken a series of steps aimed at fomenting unrest within its northwestern neighbor.

When civil strife rocked a suburb of Baku in mid-2002, local authorities made no secret of the fact that they strongly suspected clandestine Iranian involvement.[65] Officials in Baku also believe Iranian secret services are involved in financing the rise of separatist movements (such as the Islamic Party of Azerbaijan) within the former Soviet republic.[66] And Iran has commenced public outreach designed to foment separatist tendencies in Azerbaijan via illegal television and radio transmissions from broadcast outlets like Iran's *Sahar-2* television station.[67] Iran's ayatollahs "have spent a lot of money building mosques; they have sent people to teach in religious schools, they are broadcasting anti-American propaganda into the country," according to one Western diplomat.[68]

Iran's meddling was so pervasive that in the summer of 2002, Azerbaijan's then–President Haidar Aliyev complained publicly about it in an interview with the *Bakinskii Rabochii* newspaper. Aliyev's oblique reference to outside "forces" that were attempting to "create an Islamic state" was a clear allusion to Tehran's concerted efforts to spread its radical brand of Islam.[69]

Iran's activism has not stopped there, however. Over the past several years, the Islamic Republic has also begun to resettle ethnic Azeris living along the Azeri-Iranian border further inland.[70] The aim of this policy of internal displacement, according to Azeri observers, is to dilute ambitions for independence among Iran's Azeri population.

At the same time, Iran has attempted to intimidate Baku into alignment with its policies. In mid-October 2003, Iran commenced large-scale military maneuvers in its northwest, near Azerbaijan. The exercises massed troops on the Iranian-Azeri border in a clear show of force aimed at dissuading the former Soviet republic from expanding cooperation with the United States.[71]

These tactics appear to be having their desired effect. In the summer of 2004, Azeri officials unveiled plans for a new accord on religious cooperation with Iran—one that would substantially tighten religious ties between Baku and Tehran and, Iranian officials hope, pave the way for a counterweight to "the satanic triangle comprised of the United States, Britain, and Israel."[72] Subsequently, Iranian President Mohammed Khatami made a high-profile visit to Azerbaijan, signing ten agreements on joint cooperation.[73] The two countries also have substantially enhanced their security cooperation, codifying new protocols on anti-crime, counter-narcotics, and counterterrorism cooperation and opening discussions about dialogue on military and defense cooperation.[74] As these steps indicate, Azerbaijan is slowly but surely drifting toward accommodation with the Islamic Republic.

Ankara's About-Face

Perhaps Iran's most notable accomplishment, however, has been vis-à-vis its historic regional rival, Turkey.

The end of the Cold War brought with it a monumental clash of competing worldviews in the "post-Soviet space." On one side was Iran's brand of radical political theology, which officials in Tehran saw as the natural inheritor of the traditionally Muslim nations of Central Asia and the Caucasus. On the other, supported for a time by both Europe and the U.S., was the Turkish model of moderate political Islam. For Ankara, the end of the Cold War offered the opportunity to reestablish long-severed ties with the Turkic nations of Central Asia, and with Azerbaijan. And Turkish officials like Prime Minister Süleyman Demirel seized the opportunity, issuing calls for a confederation of Turkic nations to replace the U.S.S.R.[75] For their part, the United States and European nations, wary over the rising tide of Islamic fundamentalism worldwide, threw their weight behind Turkey's bid for regional supremacy.

The resulting geopolitical tug-of-war between Ankara and Tehran took many forms. The two countries articulated competing visions for regional development, and commenced grassroots efforts to promote either Pan-Shi'ism or Pan-Turkism among the fragile former Soviet states. Both also built deep trade ties to the countries of Central Asia and the Caucasus, competing for the energy resources of the Caspian Basin. The scope of this competition led some to predict that the political direction of the Caucasus and Central Asia would hinge in large part on "whether Turkey can outplay Iran."[76]

More than a decade later, it is becoming increasingly clear that that question has been settled—and settled in favor of the Islamic Republic. Indeed, over the past several years, Ankara has steadily drifted toward a new relationship with Tehran.

Much of this movement has been underpinned by energy. Turkey's growing reliance on Iran—which could provide roughly 20 percent of total Turkish natural gas consumption by the end of the decade[77]—has certainly diminished Ankara's economic leverage vis-à-vis Tehran. Moreover, this dependence is deepening; talks between the two countries are now underway on a multi-million dollar plan that would sharply boost Turkish natural gas imports from Iran.[78] At this rate, officials in Ankara may very well find themselves in the near future dancing to economic tunes played in Tehran.

Politics, however, play an important role as well. Since its assumption of power in November 2002, Turkey's Islamist Justice and Development Party (AKP) has gravitated toward closer ties with its Muslim neighbors under the guise of an "independent" foreign policy. Iran has been one of the chief beneficiaries of these overtures, and bilateral contacts and economic trade between Ankara and Tehran have ballooned.[79] This political proximity has been reinforced by common worries over Iraqi instability in the aftermath of Saddam Hussein's ouster.

Moreover, Turkish policymakers are now hard at work trying to cement these policy shifts. As part of reforms aimed at facilitating Turkey's accession to the European Union, the AKP has succeeded in trimming much of the power of its main domestic political rival—the Turkish military. Through a series of legislative maneuvers, including the transfer of Turkey's influential national security council, the *Milli Guvenlik Kurulu* (MGK), into civilian hands, the AKP has managed to substantially reorient the country's foreign policy priorities—away from partnership with the U.S. and Israel and toward accommodation with Iran.

The new political balance emerging between Ankara and Tehran was on display in July 2004, when Turkish Prime Minister Recep Tayyip Erdogan traveled to Tehran for a landmark summit with Iranian President Mohammed Khatami. Erdogan's visit, the first by a Turkish Prime Minister in close to a decade, yielded a series of accords on economic, political, and security issues. The trip also marked the culmination of Ankara and Tehran's growing convergence on two pressing foreign policy issues, terrorism and Iraq—manifested by the codification of an agreement to jointly combat both Kurdish rebels and Iranian insurgents. "Both Iran and Turkey have decided to brand the Kurdistan Worker's Party (PKK) and the People's Mujahedeen [MKO]

as terrorist groups," Iranian Deputy Interior Minister for
Security Affairs Ali Asghar Ahmadi told reporters following
the meeting.[80]

For Tehran, cementing Ankara's alignment constitutes a
major strategic coup. Competition between the two countries over the hearts and minds—and the wallets—of the
Central Asian republics is bound to continue on a number of
levels. But officials in Tehran are right to see the new strategic balance that has been struck with Ankara as one that
favors their regime.

Iran's Gain, America's Loss

In the first part of 2002, the U.S. military made an alarming
disclosure. New intelligence gathered by the Pentagon's
Central Command, then actively engaged in military operations in Afghanistan, indicated that Iran was secretly training Islamic terrorists for future operations throughout
Central Asia. According to the information gleaned by U.S.
forces, elements of the *Pasdaran* were building a terrorist
beachhead in the region, providing training and logistical
support for insurgents from the radical, al-Qaeda–affiliated
Islamic Movement of Uzbekistan (IMU), including the
group's leader, Takhir Yuldash.[81] "The Iranians are helping
to coordinate IMU activities," one American intelligence
official told the *Washington Times* newspaper.[82]

The Iran-IMU connection is a portent of things to come.
Iran's expanding economic, strategic, and political influence
in Central Asia and the Caucasus has already begun to alter
the political correlation of forces in both regions. Left unad-
dressed, these inroads threaten to undermine the durability
of the new strategic partnerships the Bush administration is
building with the countries of the "post-Soviet space," and
to undermine U.S. efforts in what has become a critical front
in the War on Terror.

Part II

Toward an American Response

CHAPTER 5

In Search of a U.S. Approach

I ran's accelerating quest for WMD, its unabated
support for international terrorism, and its rising regional ambitions in the Persian Gulf,
Caucasus, and Central Asia have put Tehran on a collision
course with American policy and U.S. interests in the greater
Middle East. Yet little in the way of strategy has emerged so
far, either at home or abroad, in response to Iran's advances.

In the U.S., the current era of policy deadlock can be
traced back to 1997, when "reformist" cleric Mohammed
Khatami strode onto the Iranian political scene. The sudden
emergence of Khatami, a relatively obscure, soft-line cleric,
as a leading contender for Iran's presidency electrified policy
makers and the mainstream media in Washington. For those
eager to engage Iran after years of diplomatic silence,
Khatami's credentials as a social reformer,[1] not to mention
his quiet campaign rhetoric about the rule of law and civil
society, were proof positive that Tehran was turning over a
more pragmatic leaf. This belief was reinforced when, less
than eight months after his landslide election as Iran's president, Khatami announced on *CNN* that it was his intention
"to benefit from the achievements and experiences of all civilizations, Western and non-Western, and to hold dialogue
with them."[2]

This "dialogue of civilizations" number worked wonders
in Washington. In response, then–Secretary of State
Madeleine Albright in the summer of 1998 famously gushed

of a "historic opportunity" to mend fences between Washington and Tehran.[3] The high hopes of the Clinton administration also made their mark on policy toward the Islamic Republic. In the spring and summer of 1996, well before Khatami's overtures, the U.S. Congress had passed— and President Bill Clinton had subsequently signed into law—the Iran-Libya Sanctions Act (ILSA). That bit of bipartisan legislation took a hard line toward Tehran, identifying "[t]he efforts of the Government of Iran to acquire weapons of mass destruction and the means to deliver them and its support of acts of international terrorism" as a threat to "the national security and foreign policy interests of the United States and those countries with which the United States shares common strategic and foreign policy objectives."[4] In response, ILSA imposed a series of sanctions, investment restrictions, and other economic curbs with the declared objective of denying Iran "the ability to support acts of international terrorism and to fund the development and acquisition of weapons of mass destruction and the means to deliver them."[5]

The consensus over ILSA, however, began to crack soon thereafter. In the spring of 1998, the Clinton administration, at least in part eager to stoke the embers of "reform" it thought it saw within the Islamic Republic, waived sanctions on three energy firms, France's Total, Russia's Gazprom, and Malaysia's Petronas, for their development of Iran's South Pars gas field in direct contravention of ILSA.[6] By the time Congress revisited the issue of Iran's quest for WMD in the late spring of that year, the idea of containment had collapsed entirely, at least within the Executive Branch. The Iran Missile Proliferation Sanctions Act, a follow-on to ILSA designed to prevent the transfer of ballistic missile components and know-how to Iran, sailed through both Houses of Congress (by a veto-proof margin of 90-4 in the Senate and 392-22 in the House of Representatives.[7]) Yet the legislation was nonetheless promptly rejected by the Clinton White

House. The reason given? That imposing "sweeping" sanctions on the enablers of Iran's ambitions to acquire WMD would "undermine the national security objectives of the United States."[8]

Instead, the administration took the wind out of the Iran Missile Proliferation Sanctions Act procedurally, imposing nominal penalties on seven Russian entities in June 1998, and three more a year later, for their assistance to Iran's ballistic missile efforts. It would not be until the spring of 2000, after two more years of wrangling with Congress, that President Clinton would finally capitulate, approving another nonproliferation act vis-à-vis Iran—one with substantially less teeth than the 1998 legislation.[9]

Similar attitudes prevailed until the end of the Clinton administration. Throughout 1999, White House officials attempted to engage the Iranian regime through a series of quiet diplomatic overtures and financial inducements. These included not only a secret August message from Clinton to Khatami seeking Iranian assistance in the investigation of the 1995 bombing of the Khobar Towers in Dahran, Saudi Arabia, but also diplomatic feelers exploring the possibility of reinstating consular relations between Washington and Tehran.[10] The Clinton administration even decided to turn a blind eye to mounting evidence of an Iranian role in the Khobar Towers bombing, which killed nineteen American servicemen. According to Louis Freeh, Clinton's FBI director, worries over the possibility of a diplomatic backlash from Tehran led White House officials to refuse even to pursue a criminal indictment identifying Iran as a sponsor of the attack, let alone contemplate more biting measures like sanctions or retaliation.[11]

These overtures, however, met with little success. In their hopes for engagement, American policy makers had seriously misunderstood the thrust of Khatami's politics. To be sure, by the sliding scale of Iran's notoriously fractious politics, Khatami was indeed a "reformer." But he was no trailblazing revolutionary, as many in the West naively believed. His candidacy for president, after all, had not raised objections among the Iranian clerical shadow government run by Supreme Leader Ali Khamenei. And Khatami had been one of only four candidates, out of 230 applicants, that had been approved by Iran's powerful Guardian Council to run for the country's highest office.[12] Official rhetoric regarding a "dialogue of civilizations" with the West, therefore, had everything to do with easing Iran's political and economic isolation, rather than with any real abandonment of the regime's guiding principles.[13] It was a change in form, not substance, plain and simple.

In this context, President George W. Bush's groundbreaking January 2002 State of the Union address was a much needed stiffening of the spine. In his speech, the president identified Iran, together with Iraq and North Korea, as part of an "axis of evil" and promised new, proactive measures designed to prevent these countries from developing WMD or supplying them to terrorists.[14]

If the announcement made waves in the U.S. and Europe, it was an even greater bombshell in Iran. There, regime opponents celebrated what they saw as America's new commitment to their cause, while clerical stalwarts angrily railed against the president's "baseless" and "imperialistic" remarks.[15] Nor were the obvious parallels to Ronald Reagan's "Evil Empire" speech, which had put the Soviet Union on notice of U.S. antagonism almost two decades earlier, lost on Iran watchers, either at home or abroad.

The high hopes of opponents of the Iranian regime were further buoyed in the months that followed. On July 12, 2002, responding to reports of widespread protests within the Islamic Republic, President Bush stressed his government's support of the Iranian people's quest for "freedoms, human rights, and opportunities."[16] In an even more hopeful sign just one month later, Zalmay Khalilzad, at that time the administration's emissary to Afghanistan, laid out what appeared to be a detailed new Iran policy. Speaking before the Washington Institute for Near East Policy, Khalilzad outlined an approach predicated not on support for particular factions within Iran, but on support of "freedom, human rights, democracy, and economic and educational opportunity."[17]

Since then, however, the Bush White House has lost much of this moral clarity. Diplomatically, it has failed to match word to deed, limiting itself to declarations of support for Iranian democracy. Worse still, some officials within the administration's own inner circle do not seem to have gotten the message. In a February 2003 interview with the *Los Angeles Times*, for example, no less senior an official than the Deputy Secretary of State at the time, Richard Armitage, took pains to differentiate between the members of the "Axis," lumping Iraq and North Korea together while taking a softer line on Iran—all on account of Iran's "democracy."[18]

The Persistence of Bad Ideas

Given this policy paralysis, it is perhaps not surprising that for almost as long as there has been an Islamic Republic, American analysts, diplomats, and scholars have been attempting to engage it. This cadre of foreign policy "realists" is as diverse as it is influential, counting among its ranks such senior statesmen as Brent Scowcroft, former National Security Advisor to the first President Bush; Zbigniew Brzezinski, National Security Advisor under President Jimmy Carter; and Robert Gates, CIA Director under two consecutive presidents, George H. W. Bush and Bill Clinton. Yet its message has been both simple and consistent: the Islamic Republic is here to stay, and Washington must reach some sort of accommodation with Iran's ayatollahs.

Over the years, the popularity of this approach has ebbed and flowed along with the currents of Middle East politics.

Recently, however, and especially since the ascent of Mohammed Khatami to power in Tehran, this group has become an increasingly vocal constituency in Washington—agitating about the overriding need for dialogue with the Islamic Republic.[19]

Significantly, it is not that advocates of this approach actually want normalization with the regime in Tehran. Some certainly do, attracted by Iran's potential energy wealth and the possibility of lucrative trade. Most, however, see engagement as the most palatable of a small number of unattractive options. Having closed the door on the possibility of regime change in Tehran, the best these policymakers can hope for is incremental behavioral change brought about by dialogue: a twenty-first century version of President Richard Nixon's "cold peace" with the Soviet Union in the late 1960s and early 1970s.

Such an approach has been tried before. With the collapse of the Soviet Union, the countries of Europe embarked upon a broad diplomatic initiative toward the Islamic Republic. That overture, dubbed "critical dialogue," was intended by European nations as a more constructive counterpoint to American efforts to isolate Iran. Launched at the European Council summit in Edinburgh in December 1992, it attempted to influence Tehran's stance on WMD, terrorism, human rights, international law, and the Israeli-Palestinian confrontation through economic incentives and "closer relations and confidence."[20]

To be sure, "critical dialogue" was not without its detractors. In mid-1996, for example, a report by Britain's Parliamentary Human Rights Group slammed Iran for its support of terrorism, and called on European capitals to scrap their engagement strategy toward Tehran.[21] But it was not until April 1997, when a German court found Iran complicit in the brutal 1992 assassination of four Kurdish dissidents, that the EU finally suspended its efforts to engage the Islamic Republic.

The damage, however, had already been done. European efforts failed to spark any meaningful policy rethink in Tehran. They did, however, manage to undermine U.S. efforts at "containment," and to provide Iran's ayatollahs with cash and international legitimacy.

Still, old habits die hard. The catastrophic failure of "critical dialogue" did little to mute Europe's yearning for engagement. Like their counterparts in Washington, officials in Europe watched the May 1997 Iranian presidential election hopefully. And Khatami's landslide victory revived optimism that Tehran might yet toe a more moderate policy line. This belief was still on display in the fall of 2002, when—amid alarming new revelations of Iran's advanced nuclear development—the EU signaled its intention to commence new negotiations with the Islamic Republic on a sweeping trade and cooperation pact, effectively reviving the "critical dialogue" concept.[22]

Just as characteristically, Europe's overtures have been roundly rebuffed. In June 2004, just seven months after French, German, and British officials succeeding in obtaining a much sought after pledge from Iran to suspend its uranium enrichment activities, officials in Tehran went back on their word, announcing plans to resume the development of advanced centrifuges.[23] A subsequent nuclear accord, inked by Iran and the EU 3 (England, France, and Germany) in late 2004, is likely to meet the same fate.

Washington has certainly not proven to be immune from this urge for engagement. The Bush administration, despite its more mature reading of Iranian intentions, has put out quiet feelers about the possibility of a sustained dialogue, however unofficial, with Iran's leaders. In April 2003, for example, reports surfaced that top U.S. officials had met in secret with Iranian emissaries ahead of Operation Iraqi Freedom in an attempt to secure a constructive role for Tehran during the military campaign against Saddam Hussein's regime.[24]

Neither were U.S. overtures limited to the Iraq war; in October 2003, Deputy Secretary of State Richard Armitage told the Senate Foreign Relations Committee that the Bush administration was willing to open "limited discussions" with the Iranian government on a range of issues that were "of mutual interest."[25] And in December 2004, when a devastating earthquake rocked the southeastern Iranian city of Bam, causing tens of thousands of casualties and sparking a major international humanitarian effort, the U.S. attempted to use disaster relief to generate new contacts with Tehran.

Such efforts, however, have met with depressing results. For all of its dulcet diplomatic tones, the Iranian theocracy remains deeply antagonistic to any sort of accommodation with the United States. This is why Iran's ayatollahs have reverted to old habits in Iraq, preferring the zero-sum approach of fomenting instability to an American foothold in their western neighbor. In similar fashion, Washington's diplomatic overtures—including its "humanitarian diplomacy" toward Tehran in the wake of the Bam disaster—have been systematically and repeatedly scuppered by clerical hard-liners antagonistic to any sort of normalization with the United States.[26]

The Limits of Diplomacy

In the face of these failures, the Bush administration—preoccupied with post-war Iraq and a plethora of domestic concerns—has so far opted to take a back seat to the international community in its approach toward Tehran. This *laissez-faire* approach has netted little tangible benefit, however. On the most pressing international issue, that of Iran's nuclear program, Tehran's atomic strides may have succeeded in generating a mounting chorus of concern on both sides of the Atlantic. But so far, they have fallen short of prompting any concrete action from the international community. And they have done nothing to address the true extent of Iran's nuclear ambitions—or the strategic challenge now posed by Islamic Republic.

Nor are they likely to in the future. Europe and the U.S. remain worlds apart on the issue of Iran's nuclear timeline. When surveyed in November 2004, officials in Paris, Brussels, and London shared the belief that the Islamic Republic remained some five to six years away from an offensive nuclear capability.[27] By contrast, the U.S.—to say nothing of its allies in the Middle East—believe that Iran could cross the nuclear threshold much sooner.[28] This difference, to a large degree, explains Europe's persistent pursuit of a diplomatic option with regard to Iran's nuclear ambitions. It also suggests that Washington and European capitals will find it extremely difficult, if not altogether impossible, to reach consensus as to the gravity and maturity of the Iranian threat.

Agreement on the broader challenge posed by Iran's strategic advances in the Persian Gulf and Central Asia is likely to be similarly elusive. The bulk of European states have little in the way of direct interests that could be threatened by Iranian activism in the Gulf, or its strategic inroads in the Caspian Basin. Even those that do tend to pay little heed to Iranian meddling in Iraq and Afghanistan, preferring pragmatic engagement with Iran's ayatollahs on issues of trade and diplomacy.

Iran, meanwhile, has positioned itself as a spoiler for American policy in the greater Middle East. And through its efforts to acquire weapons of mass destruction, its broadening foreign policy agenda, and its strategic expansion into the Persian Gulf and "post-Soviet space," Tehran has already come much of the way toward this goal.

These realities underscore the need for an independent American strategy—one capable of reassuring regional allies, deterring Iranian aggression, and curbing the Islamic Republic's expansionism. At first blush, such an effort might appear daunting. In truth, however it is hardly implausible, for many of the tools needed to tame Tehran are already at Washington's disposal.

CHAPTER 6

The Start of a Strategy

Without question, the most urgent challenge now confronting American policy makers is preventing an Iranian nuclear breakout. Already, Iran's advances have begun to alter the correlation of forces in the Middle East—much to the detriment of the U.S. and America's regional allies, which have begun to feel the corrosive global potential of an atomic Iran, ranging from a nuclear arms race in the Middle East to Tehran's growing capacity for nuclear blackmail.

So far, however, the West has had little success in altering either the pace or the direction of Iran's atomic drive. The idea of an atomic "grand bargain"—entailing Iran's abandonment of domestic uranium enrichment in favor of foreign nuclear fuel supplies—has not found much purchase in Tehran.[1] Rather, Iranian officials have insisted on their right to carry out nuclear development, and have made a point of insisting that the international community accept their country into the "nuclear club."[2]

The Problem with Preemption

Over time, the scope and gravity of this threat have led American policy makers to explore the idea of a military option against the Iranian regime. In doing so, they have been guided by the example of Israel's daring 1981 raid on

Iraq's Osiraq nuclear reactor—a preemptive strike that succeeded in setting back the Iraqi atomic effort by years, if not decades.[3]

But, as officials in Washington are discovering, Iran is not Iraq. The Iranian nuclear program today is far more complex, and more advanced, than that of Iraq at the time of the Osiraq strike. Moreover, the Islamic Republic has learned from Iraq's unfortunate experience, and over the years has put a premium on scattering, hardening, and fortifying its nuclear infrastructure. Compounding these difficulties, it is unclear how much actionable intelligence the U.S. possesses regarding the location and fortifications of existing Iranian facilities. Finally, any action perceived to be regime-threatening by Iran can be expected to be met with potentially severe retaliatory action—ranging from a blockade of the Strait of Hormuz to an increase in support for terrorism throughout the region and in the West.[4] Reflecting these considerations, a wide-ranging, realistic war-game simulation conducted by the *Atlantic Monthly* in the fall of 2004 concluded that "as a tool to slow or stop Iran's progress toward nuclear weaponry . . . the available [American] military options are likely to fail in the long term."[5]

The practical considerations surrounding military action against Iran are compounded by political ones. The U.S.-led campaign against Saddam Hussein's regime constituted the first concrete manifestation of one of the Bush administration's most significant strategic concepts—the principle of military preemption. That groundbreaking new policy, outlined in the Bush administration's September 2002 National Security Strategy, is an effort to adapt the concept of imminent threats—and the international legitimacy of a preventive response—to take into account "the capabilities and objectives of today's adversaries."[6] Since then, however, American difficulties in post-war Iraq, ranging from problems securing the peace to a failure to unearth the former regime's alleged WMD, have seriously damaged the sustainability—and the credibility—of preemption as a long-term principle. These missteps, coupled with lingering questions about when, and how, future instances of preemption are likely to occur, mean the U.S. will have far greater difficulty in marshalling domestic and international support for decisive action against Iran.

In fact, international resistance is already becoming visible, and not just from countries like France and Germany, which had originally opposed Saddam Hussein's overthrow. America's staunchest allies in the War on Terror have expressed serious misgivings about a military option against Iran. In November 2004, for example, Britain's Foreign Secretary, Jack Straw, in a clear message to Washington, took the unprecedented step of publicly ruling out the possibility of Downing Street's participation in such a military offensive. "I don't see any circumstances in which military action would be justified against Iran, full stop," Straw told reporters.[7]

Nevertheless, at least one willing participant remains. Over the past several years, Israeli military planners have viewed Iran's burgeoning strategic arsenal with mounting alarm. According to top Israeli intelligence officials, Iran's nuclear program now constitutes the single greatest "threat to the existence of Israel" since the Jewish state's founding in 1948.[8] In response, policy makers in Jerusalem have begun a substantial overhaul of their strategic deterrent. This includes accelerated work on missile defenses (from advanced testing of the Arrow theater missile defense system to the deployment of sophisticated sensors[9]), plans for a sea-based component for the country's strategic arsenal,[10] and an expansion of long-range aerial strike capabilities.[11]

Still, technical problems abound. Unlike the Osiraq raid, which targeted just one lightly defended reactor, an Israeli offensive against Iran would need to neutralize multiple, hardened facilities in order to be even partially successful. Such an endeavor would be a logistical nightmare, requiring an enormous expenditure of resources. It also is likely to be accompanied by heavy casualties.

Moreover, potential Israeli air strikes on Iran would take three likely directions—a northern route over Turkish territory; an eastern path, traversing Jordan and Iraq; or a southern trajectory, through Saudi Arabian airspace and into the Persian Gulf.[12] Given the tense political relations between Jerusalem and Riyadh, and the potential political fallout from a breach of either Jordanian or Iraqi airspace, it can be assumed that the northern route via Turkey represents the most attractive option. In the past, Israel might have been able to rely on Ankara to permit this sort of passage as part of the vibrant strategic relationship developed between the two countries over the past decade. The recent deterioration of political ties between Ankara and Jerusalem, however, has called any such calculations into question. Indeed, Turkish military planners have increasingly reoriented their strategic doctrine away from traditional state-based threats toward the challenges posed by transnational terrorism.[13] As part of this shift, officials in Ankara have expressed their opposition to a military option against the Islamic Republic, instead throwing their weight squarely behind Europe's diplomatic efforts as the preferred means of stalling Iran's nuclear progress.[14]

Israeli officials seem to recognize these harsh realities. As Yuval Steinitz, a leading legislator and chairman of the Knesset's Foreign Affairs and Defense Committee, stressed in an August 2004 interview with the *Jerusalem Post*, the West should not expect "Little Israel" to avert a crisis over Iran's nuclear program. Rather, Steinitz says, Iran "is a problem of the leaders of the civilized world."[15] Israeli Prime Minister Ariel Sharon has been even more emphatic. "Israel is not planning to attack Iran. The way to treat Iran is to exercise political and economic pressure," Sharon told the *New York Post* a month later.[16]

None of this is to say that such a strike is not possible. The political leadership in Israel may deem their interests sufficiently served by even a partial delay of Iran's atomic efforts to warrant the use of military force.[17] But the U.S. cannot bank on the possibility of another Osiraq. Neither should it embrace the idea of military action against Iran as anything other than a last resort.

A New Containment Regime

Thankfully, such a time has not yet arrived. The U.S. still has the opportunity to blunt the Islamic Republic's atomic ambitions, as well as its regional maneuvers. Doing so requires that Washington work on four distinct but related fronts:

Making Counterproliferation Matter

In May 2003, on a visit to Poland, President George W. Bush unveiled a groundbreaking new plan to prevent the spread of weapons of mass destruction. "The United States and a number of our close allies, including Poland, have begun working on new agreements to search planes and ships carrying suspect cargo and to seize illegal weapons or missile technologies," the President revealed in a public address at the Wawel Royal Castle in Krakow. "Over time, we will extend this partnership as broadly as possible to keep the world's most destructive weapons away from our shores and out of the hands of our common enemies."[18]

Since then, that effort—the U.S.-led Proliferation Security Initiative (PSI)—has become a pivotal international partnership. Building on the principles outlined in the Bush administration's National Security Strategy, it embraces the notion that preventive action is necessary to keep rogue states and terrorists from acquiring catastrophic capabilities. From its original eleven "core" members—Australia, France, Germany, Italy, Japan, the Netherlands, Poland, Portugal, Spain, the United Kingdom, and the U.S.—the PSI is now supported in one form or another by over sixty nations, including Russia. Its activities, ranging from aggressive intelligence sharing to the interdiction and seizure of suspect vessels, have succeeded in effectively curtailing much of North Korea's illicit proliferation activities, including not only its active missile trade—the single largest source of revenue for the regime of North Korean dictator Kim Jong-Il—but its drug trafficking and commercial smuggling as well.

Even more significantly, the PSI can be credited with Libyan leader Moammar Gadhafi's abrupt about-face on weapons of mass destruction. The successful September 2003 interception of a German-flagged ship, the *BBC China*, carrying nuclear centrifuges bound for the North African state—and the subsequent, credible threat of punitive action from the U.S.—convinced Tripoli to reverse course and give up its pursuit of nuclear and ballistic missile know-how.[19] In the process, it has handed the Bush administration its greatest counterproliferation success to date.

The White House has moved to capitalize on these gains. In February 2004, in an address before the National Defense University in Washington, President Bush outlined a series of new counterproliferation proposals designed in part to expand the PSI's role and functions.[20] As part of the President's vision, the PSI will continue to grow in scope to target both WMD networks and proliferation facilitators, such as the notorious A.Q. Khan nuclear cartel in Pakistan. Members of the Initiative will also step up law enforcement coordination and strengthen their respective domestic legal authorities to better address illegal proliferation activities.[21]

These priorities suggest that the PSI (as well as other, related counterproliferation initiatives) can and should be adapted to more comprehensively address the contemporary threat from the Islamic Republic. Through closer coordination with like-minded states in the Persian Gulf and Eastern Mediterranean, the U.S. has the opportunity to replicate its counterproliferation successes in the Middle East. With the help of regional allies, the U.S. can stem Iran's acquisition of WMD and missile technology from foreign suppliers, and constrain its proliferation of these technologies to both aspiring weapons-states and terrorist groups.

Containing Iran in the Caspian

The PSI is hardly the only tool in Washington's arsenal, however. In the Caucasus and Central Asia, the U.S. military is quietly moving ahead with "Caspian Guard," an innovative initiative designed to bolster regional security through expanded maritime patrols, aerial and naval surveillance, and border protections.

As part of this effort, the United States has invested deeply in strengthening Azerbaijan's counterproliferation capabilities, signing a January 2004 accord committing $10 million to the country's border security and communications infrastructure.[22] Washington and Baku have also carried out a series of joint military exercises in the Caspian Sea aimed at bolstering maritime security in the Caspian.[23] And Pentagon planners have begun discussions with their Azeri counterparts regarding cooperative military training with— and even the possible basing of American forces in—the former Soviet republic.[24]

A similar dialogue is underway with Kazakhstan. Under a five-year defense accord signed in 2003, the United States has bankrolled the construction of a Kazakh military base in the Caspian coast city of Atyrau, and has allocated millions of dollars to provide equipment and training for the Central Asian state's army, maritime, and border-patrol forces.[25] Since late 2003, the United States, working via the North Atlantic Treaty Organization (NATO) and in tandem with Russia, has also been engaged in a cooperative venture to create a naval force for Kazakhstan. That effort—which includes the training of marines, the emplacement of coastal artillery and the creation of a fleet of patrol craft and warfighting vessels[26]—is intended to assist the energy-rich Central Asian nation in better securing its sector of the Caspian.

Supplemental efforts—ranging from enhancements to Georgia's counterterrorism and border patrol capabilities to plans for joint force exercises and cooperative pipeline security with Armenia and Uzbekistan—are also underway.[27]

The goal of these efforts is clear: to fashion a security regime in a region sorely in need of one through investments in border protection, military capabilities and intelligence-sharing. But, if properly harnessed and expanded, Caspian Guard could also turn out to be much more—a way to contain and defuse the threat Iran now poses to the countries of the "post-Soviet space," and to American interests there.[28]

One such step is immediately apparent. Moscow and Washington are already invested in the creation of a regional naval force for Astana, the primary goal of which will be the protection of regional energy sources from power grabs—in and of itself an important tool against Iran, which has in the past attempted just this sort of activity.[29] But a more ambitious regional role for this fleet is possible as well. Outfitted with the proper technologies, of either American or Russian origin, Kazakhstan's naval contingent could serve as a hedge against Iranian ballistic missiles targeting Europe.

Such a move would be imminently practical. After all, the vast majority of Iranian missiles fired toward EU nations from Iranian territory would pass over the Caspian.[30] Moreover, it would be politically prudent. The United States already has a vested interest in protecting its NATO partners from harm. For Russia, such an initiative should also be an attractive option. By helping in the deployment of Caspian defenses against Iranian missiles, Moscow would position itself as a guarantor of security for much of the European Union.

Through this and other measures, the United States has a real ability to curtail Iran's capacity to threaten either its allies in Europe, or its emerging strategic partners in the "post-Soviet space."

Reviving Gulf Defense

Over the past several years, fears of a rising Tehran—and the gradual retraction of the American strategic umbrella from the region—have begun to drive many of the countries of the Persian Gulf toward an accommodation with the Islamic Republic. The results have been dramatic; through a series of sweeping military and strategic accords codified quietly over the past four years, Iran has succeeded in bringing many of the Gulf states under its influence.

Cooperation, however, does not necessarily mean collusion. For many of these countries, partnership with Tehran remains a product of necessity—a function of the inadequacy of national defenses and regional alliances in addressing Iran's rising expansionism. Distrust of Iran still runs very deep. As an October 2003 editorial in London's influential Arab-language *Al-Sharq Al-Awsat* newspaper emphasized, Iran now poses a threat to "Saudi Arabia, Oman, Iraq, Afghanistan, Turkmenistan, and Azerbaijan, which share with Iran a land border of 5,400 km and a sea border of 2,400 km. . . . The Iranian nuclear danger threatens us, first and foremost, more than it threatens the Israelis and the Americans."[31]

Such worries have prompted regional states to explore methods by which to neutralize Iran's growing potential for nuclear blackmail. In 2003, the six-member Gulf Cooperation Council (GCC), which encompasses Saudi Arabia, Kuwait, Oman, Qatar, Bahrain, and the United Arab Emirates, initiated a feasibility study to explore the creation of an alliance-wide anti-missile system.[32] GCC members have also ramped up their missile defense cooperation with the United States. In June 2004, for example, the six states held cooperative exercises with U.S. forces to coordinate responses to a potential ballistic missile threat to the Arabian Peninsula. The drills, dubbed "Eagle Resolve-2004," focused on strengthening regional missile defenses against "a simulated ballistic missile attack from the eastern and south-eastern side of the gulf"—a thinly-veiled reference to Iran.[33]

Individual GCC members, meanwhile, have accelerated their efforts to find local antidotes to the Iranian threat. The United Arab Emirates have stepped up their search for low- and medium-tier missile defenses capable of protecting against regional threats like the Iranian *Shahab-3*. When surveyed in 2003, Abu Dhabi, which traditionally has had a contentious relationship with Tehran, had begun assessing acquisition of both the Russian S-400 "Triumph" and the U.S. PAC-3 theater missile defense systems.[34] Kuwait has done the same; in late 2003, officials in Kuwait City opened discussions regarding the acquisition of a $1 billion sea- and ground-based air defense system with three unidentified defense contractors. The new system will supplement the country's existing air defense network, which consists of units of the U.S. PAC-2 and HAWK systems, as well as the Egyptian *Al Amoun*.[35] Bahrain, for its part, has approved a program to induct Patriot batteries into the country's air defenses, and, since mid-2004, has been actively working to acquire sophisticated mobile solid-state radars capable of tracking short- and medium-range missile threats.[36]

All this suggests that a variety of strategic initiatives may find fertile soil. On the one hand, a deepening of Washington's bilateral military dialogue and defense contacts with individual Gulf nations might lessen regional dependence not only on Iran, but on an increasingly volatile and unpredictable Saudi Arabia as well.[37] On the other, the creation of a formal American security architecture over the region could reinvigorate Washington's regional partnerships while excluding and isolating the Islamic Republic.[38]

Underpinning each of these steps, however, should be the understanding that renewed deterrence and defense is critical to preserving American alliances in the Persian Gulf. Already, Tehran's burgeoning strategic capabilities have begun to undermine Washington's foothold in the region, and to separate American partners from the United States in favor of a *modus vivendi* with Iran. Future engagement, therefore, requires that the United States provide Tehran's neighbors with the tools to counter its growing potential for nuclear and ballistic missile blackmail—and to strengthen regional allies who might eventually have to live with a nuclear Iran.

Engaging New Allies

None of these efforts are likely to succeed without international support. If the difficult diplomatic experience of the recent past is any indication, however, rallying Europe to the side of a hard-line American approach toward the Islamic Republic is likely to be a tall order. Instead, the United States would do well to look elsewhere in its efforts to fashion an international policy consensus in favor of Iran's isolation.

The most critical element of such an approach is undoubtedly Moscow. Since the start of the Russo-Iranian entente over a decade ago, Russia has been the country most directly responsible for Iran's reemergence as a major player in the Middle East. For just as long, American officials have been attempting to engage, cajole, and pressure the Kremlin into rolling back its assistance to Iran's ayatollahs. So far, these efforts have been spectacularly ineffective; officials in Moscow have consistently preferred to nurture their strategic ties with Tehran over cooperating with Washington.

Now, however, new signs suggest that the United States could find great benefit in renewed engagement with Russia on the issue of Iran. For one thing, Russian WMD proliferation to Iran over the past decade has been driven in large part by the belief in the Kremlin that such activity was essentially a cost-free exercise. This is no longer the case; Tehran's heavy investments in nuclear and ballistic missile technologies have reaped substantial rewards, and dramatically expanded the threat the Islamic Republic now poses to Russia. According to informed estimates, at its current rate of development Iran is on track to field a nuclear-capable medium-range rocket by 2006—making it capable of threatening some twenty million people in the south of Russia, Kazakhstan, and Ukraine.[39] This threat is becoming recognized by a growing number of Russian politicians, who have begun to speak publicly about the Iranian strategic threat to Russia.[40]

For another, Iran's strategic ambitions increasingly jeopardize Russian interests in the Middle East. With the removal of Saddam Hussein's regime, Tehran has invested considerable sums of money in perpetuating instability in Iraq via an insurgency that has in part threatened Russian citizens now working within the country. Iran has also demonstrated growing designs over Iraq's energy sector, and has announced plans to exploit shared resources with or without the acquiescence of the new Iraqi government.[41] This is sure to adversely affect Russian companies, which are now negotiating with the Iraqi leadership for a reestablishment of their role within the former Ba'athist state.

Finally, the Russian-Iranian understanding in the "post-Soviet space" could soon become a thing of the past. Worries over the possibility of Iranian support for radical separatism in Russia's turbulent "Southern Rim" were at the core of Russian-Iranian contacts a decade ago. Back then, Moscow moved quickly—and successfully—to secure Tehran's good behavior in exchange for arms and nuclear assistance. But Iran's hands-off approach in the Caucasus cannot be assumed to be indefinite. The Islamic Republic might be tempted to use the possibility of support for Chechen insurgents (or other regional radicals) as a blackmail tool against

Russia, particularly if it feels threatened by Russia's strides toward Europe or the U.S., or if it would like to blunt international pressure over its nuclear program. Someday, therefore, Moscow might no longer find itself in the driver's seat of its relationship with Tehran.

As a result of these dynamics, Washington soon could notice a much more constructive tenor to its long-running dialogue with Moscow over the Iranian nuclear program. The Bush administration is well positioned to capitalize on these changes, provided it can avoid the mistakes made over Iraq. In the run-up to that conflict, senior American statesmen and government officials tried repeatedly, and unsuccessfully, to secure Russia's support for U.S. military action. These policy makers had reason to be optimistic; after years of heavy investment, Russia had emerged as the largest shareholder in Iraq's energy sector, with concessions estimated at between $7 and $30 billion.[42] Kremlin officials also had not given up hope on recovering Iraq's massive Cold War–era debt to Moscow (as much as $12 billion, when adjusted for inflation).[43] Policy makers in Washington therefore believed Russia had a hefty financial stake in securing a seat at the post-Saddam planning table.

But while U.S. emissaries were pledging continued Russian access to Iraqi oil, Iraq's opposition groups were sending a different signal. In public and private statements, Iraqi opposition figures made clear that they intended to punish Russia for its long-standing support of the regime in Baghdad.[44] Without the commitment of those factions, Russian officials were forced to conclude that their investments in Iraq would likely be lost.

This experience is instructive. After all, the U.S. understands that Russia has deep and lucrative investments within the Islamic Republic, and that cooperation with Iran is vital to several of Russia's struggling industries. Policy makers in Washington must therefore emphasize that they do not seek a Russo-Iranian divorce. Rather, they should stress the tangible political and economic benefits to Russia of a harder line vis-à-vis Tehran in the Middle East and its Near Abroad—and of the dangers to Moscow that would be posed by a nuclear Iran. In doing so, they will lay the groundwork for collaboration with the Kremlin on the rollback of the current clerical regime in Tehran, and its replacement with a pragmatic secular one.

A similar opening is visible in Ankara. Ties between the United States and Turkey have been tepid since Ankara's unexpected refusal to grant basing rights to American troops on the eve of the spring 2003 Iraq campaign—a move that torpedoed U.S. plans for a northern front against Saddam Hussein's regime. Since then, however, policy makers in both countries have begun to mend fences. In the fall of 2003, Turkey agreed to an American request to contribute troops to Iraqi stability operations.[45] And Turkish politicians, including Prime Minister Recep Tayyip Erdogan, have made considerable efforts to engage the United States in dialogue over topics like Cyprus, Iraqi reconstruction, and counterterrorism.[46] Yet it is in a different, and largely unexplored, context—as a hedge against Iranian ambitions in the Caucasus and Central Asia—that Turkey can provide its most important contribution.

Turkey's historic role as a strategic competitor of Iran has eroded considerably in recent times as a result of a number of economic, political, and strategic factors. Nevertheless, the emerging Turkish-Iranian entente is likely to prove anything but durable. Profoundly divergent strategic priorities on everything from Central Asian Islam to Caspian energy to the future political composition of post-war Iraq suggest that Ankara and Tehran will remain more competitors than partners in the long run. Indeed, Ankara's deep ethnic and historical ties to the countries of the Caucasus and Central Asia make it a natural counterweight to Iranian-sponsored religious radicalism in those regions. Given its deep interest in expanding trade and development in the Caspian, Turkey also remains antagonistic to Iran's expanding regional maneuvers there. Additionally, Tehran's ongoing sponsorship of terrorism has put Iran and Turkey on very different sides of the War on Terror. These commonalities suggest that Turkey's most constructive role might just be as a force multiplier for American interests in what some observers have called its "northern neighborhood."[47]

Turkey's potential utility does not stop there. Given its broad historic ties to Pakistan, Ankara could even prove to be an important interlocutor in convincing Islamabad to curtail nuclear proliferation to the Islamic Republic.

In light of these realities, strengthening the U.S.-Turkish relationship—and articulating a more active Turkish role in curbing the international threat posed by Iran—is likely to rebound to the benefit of both Washington and Ankara.

A Window of Opportunity

Such a game plan is sorely needed. Iran's nuclear progress and its rising foreign policy adventurism have already begun to alter the geopolitical landscape of the Persian Gulf and the "post-Soviet space." Through a strategy that successfully bolsters the Islamic Republic's vulnerable regional neighbors, rolls back its military advances, and curbs access to critical WMD technologies, the United States can do much to delay and temper the gathering threat from Tehran. Ultimately, however, these measures must be just a prelude to a more far-reaching approach—one aimed at bringing about the end of the current regime in Tehran.

Such an idea is hardly new. The CIA-sponsored coup that removed Iranian Prime Minister Mohammed Mossadeq from power in 1953 can be correctly classified as an early instance of regime change. But in recent years, the idea of regime transformation has fallen by the wayside, and official Washington has embraced the goal of behavioral modification among Iran's ayatollahs as the desired objective of U.S.

policy. It is now exceedingly clear, however, that this incremental approach has become downright dangerous, both for American interests and for the security of Iran's neighbors.

The implications are clear. If it is serious about the long-term success of its strategy in the greater Middle East, the United States must seek a fundamental transformation in the character of the Iranian regime itself. When it does, American policy makers will find no shortage of attention among the Iranian people.

CHAPTER 7

Iranians for Regime Change

During the fall of 2002, a remarkable event took place in Iran. The country's parliament, or *majles*, in an effort to capitalize on the wave of anti-Americanism sweeping the region, and as a way of shoring up its own anti-Western policies, commissioned an official poll to survey national attitudes toward the United States. The outcome was supposed to be predetermined—a resounding vote in favor of Tehran's continued antagonism toward Washington, and a renewed mandate for the Islamic Revolution at home and abroad.

But Iran's leaders found out that they should be careful what they wish for. Fully 74 percent of the approximately 1,500 Iranians surveyed by three different polling institutes, including Iran's quasi-official National Institute for Research Studies and Opinion Polls, supported the idea of dialogue with the United States.[1] And less than eight months after President Bush had labeled their country part of an "Axis of Evil," nearly half of those polled affirmed that Washington's policy toward Iran was "to some extent correct."[2] All in all, it was a resounding defeat for Iran's ruling theocracy.

The results of the September 2002 survey provide a telling glimpse into the sorry state of affairs within Iran. Just over two and a half decades after the Islamic Revolution, the country is nothing short of a failed state. Half of its sixty-nine million population lives below the poverty line.[3] A fifth is unemployed, and 1.4 million youths join its ranks every year.[4] Inflation stands at around 25 percent, while per capita income is at pre-Revolutionary levels (some $1,800 per year).[5] Corruption has decayed virtually every sector of the government and the economy.[6] Prostitution and drug abuse are rampant, with teenage addiction rates five times higher than those of the United States.[7]

Moreover, conditions worsened under the rule of Mohammed Khatami. Despite his public calls for domestic reforms and a "dialogue of civilizations" with the West, Iran's "reformist" president presided over a full-bore assault on freedom of expression and political dissent. Since 2001, the Iranian regime has shut down more than one hundred newspapers and imprisoned dozens of opposition journalists.[8] This led the international media watchdog Reporters Without Borders, in its 2004 annual report, to dub Iran "the biggest prison for journalists in the Middle East."[9] At the same time, numerous pieces of legislation passed by the *majles*—on such topics as judicial freedoms, police procedures, and international humanitarian standards—remain unratified.[10] These conditions led the UN General Assembly to formally express "serious concern" about the "continuing violations of human rights" in Iran in December 2004.[11]

It is perhaps not surprising, therefore, that the country's political consensus has begun to crumble. In July 2002, the Ayatollah Jalaleddin Taheri, a stalwart of the old regime, unexpectedly resigned from his post as the Imam of Isfahan. Taheri's letter of resignation, circulated widely in the Iranian press, blasted the "failed" policies of the current regime for the country's "unemployment, inflation and high prices, the hellish gap between poverty and wealth, the deep and daily-growing distance between the classes, the stagnation and decline of national revenue, a sick economy, bureaucratic corruption, desperately weak administrators, the growing flaws in the country's political structure, embezzlement, bribery and addiction."[12] Taheri is not alone; other Iranian clerics and intellectuals have since followed suit, publicly breaking with the policies of the regime in Tehran to call for a new national political balance.[13]

Even the regime's enforcers no longer seem to be immune from doubts. In February 2003, the London-based *Al Sharq al-Awsat* disclosed that three top Iranian security officials had recently defected from the Islamic Republic, taking with them a trove of documents, video recordings, and personnel files.[14] Those who have stayed, meanwhile, appear increasingly disaffected. During the student protests that shook Iran in the summer of 2003, the regime was forced to recruit hundreds of Arab mercenaries for their clampdown on dissent.[15] Apparently, Tehran's mullahs can no longer even trust the loyalty of their own enforcers.

Just as significantly, Iran is in the throes of a demographic and ideological upheaval. Fully two-thirds of the Iranian population is under the age of thirty, and half is under age twenty.[16] Most Iranians, therefore, have lived nearly all of their lives under the Islamic Revolution, and are painfully aware of its shortcomings. Not coincidentally, they are among the only truly pro-American populations in the region. In the days after 9/11, as throngs celebrated in other parts of the Muslim world, hundreds of Iranians took to the streets to express their solidarity with the United States.[17] They did so again in November 2002, in a nationwide series of student protests with many manifestations but one unifying theme: "Death to the Taliban, in Kabul and in Tehran."[18] The scope of this opposition is breathtaking. Between March 2002 and March 2003, more than a thousand anti-regime protests are estimated to have taken place throughout Iran.[19]

Communication Breakdown

For the United States, Iran's youthful, pro-Western population represents an indispensable constituency. After all, one of the Bush administration's most enduring challenges in the War on Terror has been effectively communicating its goals and objectives to a skeptical Muslim world. Since 9/11, this imperative has spawned a frenetic American public diplomacy effort—including media outreach by top administration officials—aimed at winning hearts and minds in the Middle East.

Yet Iran has figured only belatedly in these plans. More than nine months after September 11th, and with American officials appearing repeatedly on Arabic networks like *al-Jazeera*, not one high-ranking U.S. official had yet attempted to make the case for the "Bush Doctrine" on Iranian radio or television, despite the availability of numerous foreign broadcasting outlets capable of effectively carrying their message.[20]

Even when the U.S. government did finally attempt to correct this omission, the results fell far short of adequate. In December 2002, with much fanfare, the U.S. Broadcasting Board of Governors launched its new 24-hour-a-day Farsi-language broadcasting vehicle, *Radio Farda*.[21] Quickly, however, the station's entertainment-driven format unleashed a barrage of criticism. The United States, observers in both the Congress and the media said, had diluted its democratic message.[22] Since then, broadcasting to Iran has languished, despite Congressional attempts to expand outreach.[23]

The lackluster nature of this effort is symptomatic of a larger malaise within the U.S. government—confusion about exactly whom within the Iranian regime to engage. Ever since Khatami's May 1997 election, hopes for contact with more moderate elements of Tehran's clerical establishment have persisted in official Washington. These yearnings have squelched any real progress in the quest for alternatives to the current regime in Tehran. Iran's ayatollahs, for their part, have nurtured this inertia, permitting the veneer of pluralism (but no real progress) in Iran's domestic political debate. The result? No American strategy, and a policy vulnerable to Tehran's manipulation.

Such disarray can have devastating consequences. This became clear in the summer of 2003, when a renewed resurgence of anti-regime protests rocked the Islamic Republic. Over the course of several weeks, thousands of protesters took to the streets of Tehran and other Iranian cities, rallied by foreign broadcasting outlets like the Los Angeles-based National Iranian Television (NITV). Unable to curtail such foreign broadcasting itself, Iran turned to Fidel Castro's Cuba. Within days, Havana began using a Russian-built electronic warfare facility to jam both U.S. government and private broadcasts into the Islamic Republic.[24] The interference eliminated a crucial outlet for political information and organization for Iranian protesters, effectively neutralizing the nascent democratic protests at a critical time, when they had begun spreading across the country. A stunned American official likened the jamming to an "act of war."[25]

Yet a robust American response failed to materialize. The administration brushed aside the significance of the satellite jamming, and did nothing to demonstrate to Iran's ayatollahs—and to their comrades-in-arms abroad—that such interference carries serious consequences. In the process, Washington telegraphed a distinct message: there are limits to America's support of the Iranian people's urge for democracy.

The Reagan Doctrine Revisited

Reversing this trend requires the United States to utilize public diplomacy as part of a larger political warfare strategy—one designed to engage and empower the Iranian population vis-à-vis the clerical regime.

Such an idea is not new. During the Cold War, the United States relied heavily on public diplomacy, via organs like the Voice of America, the United States Information Agency (USIA), and Radio Free Europe, to pierce the Iron Curtain and export American ideals to the Soviet Bloc. Perhaps the most ardent proponent of this war of ideas against the U.S.S.R. was President Ronald Reagan. On his watch, efforts to spread American values abroad were strengthened significantly through the creation of new institutions like the National Endowment for Democracy and new broadcasting outlets such as Radio Marti, as well as through major infusions of funding.[26]

The results were dramatic. At the height of their Cold War popularity, America's premier public diplomacy vehicles—the Voice of America, Radio Free Europe, and Radio Liberty—reached up to 80 percent of the population of Eastern Europe, and half of the citizens of the Soviet Union, every week.[27] And the message they carried empowered, inspired, and motivated a generation of leaders in the Soviet Bloc, ranging from Czechoslovakia's future president, Vaclav Havel, to the U.S.S.R.'s most prominent dissident and Nobel Laureate, Andrei Sakharov.[28] The direct impact of American public diplomacy was visible in such places as Poland, where U.S. support spurred the emergence of Lech Walesa's *Solidarnosc* (Solidarity) movement in the early 1980s.

Since the end of the Cold War, however, the United States has all but abdicated public diplomacy as a vehicle by which to engage the outside world. Through a series of steps during the 1990s—from steep cuts for broadcast staffing funds to the reduction of cultural exchange programs—America's tools of outreach were systematically eviscerated and politicized. The culmination came in October 1999, with the formal elimination of the USIA as a freestanding governmental agency as part of new legislation aimed at restructuring and streamlining the nation's public diplomacy effort.

More than half a decade later, this trend has not been reversed. When surveyed close to a year and a half after September 11th, the United States was still spending, in real terms, about one-third less on public diplomacy than it did during the Cold War—notwithstanding an acute need to inform a massive base of "undecided" citizens in the Arab and Muslim world about American objectives and values.[29] Just as significantly, the message of American public diplomacy has effectively been neutered through programmatic changes that have placed a premium on popular music (and a smattering of news reporting) at the expense of hard-hitting democracy coverage designed to empower and educate listeners the world over.[30] These sad facts led President Bush's blue-ribbon panel on public diplomacy, chaired by former U.S. Ambassador to Syria Edward Djerejian, to charge in its October 2003 report that

> a process of unilateral disarmament in the weapons of advocacy over the last decade has contributed to widespread hostility toward Americans and left us vulnerable to lethal threats to our interests and our safety. In this time of peril, public diplomacy is absurdly and dangerously under-funded.[31]

As this and numerous other studies on U.S. public diplomacy concluded since September 11th have made clear,[32] American efforts need a renewed strategic direction, additional resources and, most of all, a serious commitment to winning the battle of ideas in the larger War on Terror. And there is no better place to start than Iran, a country in the midst of massive demographic and ideological change. With the proper political will, the United States has the ability to quickly generate a robust, effective public diplomacy effort aimed at empowering Iran's young, Western-looking population.

In practical terms, doing so requires

Expanding and optimizing existing outreach. In 2004, broadcasting to Iran accounted for about 2.5 percent of the entire $577 million budget of the U.S. Broadcasting Board of Governors (BBG), and just over 1 percent of the combined $1.17 billion public diplomacy budget of the State Department and the BBG.[33] Put another way, the United

States spends under twenty-two cents *per Iranian per year* on outreach to the Islamic Republic—less than one-third of what the U.S. was spending per capita on broadcasting into the Soviet Bloc two decades ago.[34]

These meager resources fail to properly appreciate Iran's geopolitical importance, and the fact that broadcasting into the Islamic Republic requires an entirely new language set and different regional/cultural expertise than analogous efforts directed toward the Arab countries of the region. Both facts dictate that the United States should match its political interest in Iranian democracy with the financial investment necessary to make its outreach as effective as possible.

A reconfiguration of programming is also in order. Hard-hitting political analysis and coverage of current events currently account for one-quarter or less of the regular programming on America's premier public diplomacy outlet to the Islamic Republic, Radio Farda.[35] The rest is taken up by lengthy broadcasts of popular music.[36] Such a schedule is surely designed to appeal to Iran's young, Western-oriented population—an audience base that now numbers close to fifty million. Yet it would be a safe bet to say that a good portion of these young Iranians, struggling to define themselves under the corrupt, dictatorial rule of the regime in Tehran, want to hear about freedoms and personal liberties at least as much as they yearn for the latest *Top 40* offerings. The United States should make it a priority to allow them to do so.

Financing external broadcasting sources. In its quest to win Iranian hearts and minds, the United States has a powerful ally on its side: the Iranian expatriate community. The Persian diaspora in the United States now stands at over two million, making it the largest such Iranian community in the world.[37] Over time, this vibrant, politically active segment of the U.S. population has charted substantial public diplomacy gains of its own in Iran via outlets like NITV and KRSI "Radio Sedaye Iran," located in Beverly Hills.

U.S. Public Broadcasting Toward Iran

	Radio Farda	VOA Persian Service (Radio)	VOA Persian Service (Television)
Schedule	24 hours a day, 7 days a week (24/7 on mediumwave from the UAE and Kuwait; 21 hours a day on shortwave from various stations in Europe and Asia; streaming Internet broadcasts)	4 hours a day, 7 days a week (Broadcast on shortwave from various stations in Europe and Asia; mediumwave out of Kuwait launched in 2003)	4 hours per week (Simulcast on radio and direct-to-home satellite; streaming Internet broadcasts)
		VOA Persian website contains original features, updated daily, on human rights and democracy in Iran	
Programming Content	Contemporary Western and Iranian pop music (approx. 75 percent) Live newscasts; news shows; current events roundtables (approx. 25 percent)	News; interviews; call-in shows; current events roundtables	Weekly 90-minute news and information program Weekly 30-minute youth magazine show Nightly 30-minute newsmagazine show (launched July 2003) Monthly democracy promotion program (planned 2005)
Budget		$16.4 million combined (projected 2005)	

Sources: Broadcasting Board of Governors, *Broadcasting to Iran Fact Sheet*, June 16, 2003; Broadcasting Board of Governors, *BBG Broadcasting to Iran*, January 4, 2005.

So far, the U.S. government has done little to shore up these independent voices. In fact, when efforts to do so have emerged—notably, in the form of legislation like the 2003 "Iran Democracy Act" proposed by Senator Sam Brownback (R-KS)[38]—they have fallen victim to legislative infighting and conflicting political agendas.[39] These failures constitute a critical oversight, since the broadcasting efforts of Iranian expatriate elements have proven to be more effective than anything the United States has brought to bear on the public diplomacy front vis-à-vis Iran (in part by virtue of their known and beloved newscasters, actors, and entertainers, who are household names in Iran, and are certainly viewed by Iranians as more politically independent than employees of the U.S. government). This is a lapse the administration should rectify in short order.

Funding complimentary public diplomacy and political warfare mechanisms. If the high-profile organs of American public diplomacy like Voice of America and Radio Free Europe have declined in stature and reach since the end of the Cold War, subsidiary initiatives have fared even worse. Between 1991 and 2001, the number of academic and cultural exchanges between the United States and foreign nations was slashed by nearly 40 percent (from 45,000 to 29,000 annually) and the profile of American information centers abroad was scaled down dramatically.[40] All this has taken its toll, leaving the United States unable to effectively counteract the negative media image of America that now permeates Arabic broadcasting (like the Doha-based *Al-Jazeera* and Hezbollah's dedicated *Al-Manar* television station) at the grassroots level. And the likelihood of a repeat performance of the Cold War successes of such programs—which exposed leaders like Anwar Sadat and Helmut Kohl to the American message early in their political careers, and helped to instill in them an understanding of U.S. values—has been substantially reduced.

The resuscitation of such initiatives toward Iran is especially vital, given the age of the Iranian population and their increasingly evident discontent with the current clerical regime. Exposure to the American message, and to their counterparts in the United States, via cultural outreach and delegation visits could help further loosen the ideological bonds between the Iranian people and Iran's ayatollahs.

In order to increase its effectiveness, direct public broadcasting should also be buttressed by practical measures aimed at engaging the Islamic Republic's nascent democratic opposition. These steps—from the dissemination of pro-American literature and audio recordings to the provision of resources for hard-hitting opposition research and reporting on the human rights abuses of the current regime—would allow the United States to communicate more effectively with opponents of Tehran's bankrupt clerical rule, give those same elements greater international voice, and help them to network among themselves at home and abroad.

Deterring foreign interference. As its summer 2003 collaboration with Cuba eloquently demonstrated, Iran today is aided by a number of international partners who have a stake in preserving the current regime's hold on power. To these nations, Washington must demonstrate, both in word and in deed, that meddling with American public diplomacy toward the Islamic Republic will not be tolerated, and will prompt serious political and economic consequences. Only by deterring outside interference with its public diplomacy (via diplomatic, political, and economic measures, including biting sanctions if necessary) can the United States hope to empower sustainable, long-term resistance to the regime in Tehran.

There is sound basis to expect success. After all, Iran is not North Korea, a "hermit kingdom" with few tangible and durable links to the outside world. On the whole, Iranians are well educated, politically sophisticated, and socially informed. A concerted American public diplomacy campaign will provide a much-needed sign that the United States is committed to democracy in Iran, and serve as a catalyst for change among the Islamic Repubic's increasingly restive population.

Wanted: Iranian Leadership

Public diplomacy alone is not enough, however. In tandem with its efforts to engage the current of counter-revolution now visible within the Islamic Republic, the United States must find and nurture viable alternatives to the current regime in Tehran.

This promises to be a difficult undertaking. Unlike the Polish opposition to the Soviet Union in its day, Iranians are still in search of their Lech Walesa—a charismatic, populist leader to serve as the public face of their resistance. No such figure has emerged in Iran, in part because Iran's ayatollahs have given priority in recent years to brutally suppressing potential challengers, imprisoning regime opponents, and breaking up student political groups. (A case in point was the bloody clampdown on the 1999 student protests in Tehran by police and paramilitary forces). Just as significantly, they have empowered the rise of political "moderates" which nonetheless cleave to the Islamic revolutionary line. These efforts have had their desired effect, preventing the emergence of a consistent, recognizable opposition leadership within Iran.

Some alternatives have surfaced outside the confines of the regime, however—most prominently Reza Pahlavi, the son of the deposed Shah, in the United States, and the opposition *Mujahideen-e Khalq* (MKO), now headquartered in Paris. Each, however, carries its own political baggage. The true level of support among the Iranian population for Pahlavi, for all his charisma, remains unclear, despite his efforts to articulate his vision for a post-theocratic Iran.[41] The MKO, for its part, is still struggling with the terrorist label affixed to it by the Clinton administration in 1997. Notably, the Marxist group has taken significant strides toward rehabilitation, signing a voluntary disarmament agreement with Coalition forces in post-war Iraq in July 2004, in exchange for which the organization has been granted the status of "protected persons" under the Geneva Conventions by the United States.[42]

Washington now has some hard choices to make. It must either decide to harness these forces, or to seek new ones. To help in its deliberations, some practical steps are available. Grassroots polling of Iranians regarding their views on dissidents like Reza Pahlavi, carried out both officially, via governmental organs such as the Voice of America or Radio Farda, and unofficially, through independent Iranian journalists and activists, is likely to provide an accurate barometer of the popularity of these forces within the Islamic Republic—and guidance for Washington about the suitability of these elements as regime alternatives. As for the MKO, the White House would do well to rectify the discrepancy in the group's current legal status—under which it is simultaneously accorded international humanitarian protections under the laws of war, but remains a Foreign Terrorist Organization under U.S. law (a designation which places it outside the purview of the Geneva Conventions). Only then will Washington be able to determine whether it is feasible—or even desirable—for the MKO to assume a seat at the U.S. policy planning table.

A Vision of Victory

Ever since its publication in September 2002, the Bush administration's National Security Strategy has generated an extraordinary amount of controversy. Critics of White House policy from across the political spectrum have attacked the soundness of the document's strategic centerpiece, the doctrine of preemption, and raised questions about its first practical application, the war in Iraq. Yet it is in another arena entirely—that of democracy promotion—that the "Bush doctrine" could have its most far-reaching successes. "The United States," the National Security Strategy proudly proclaims, "must defend liberty and justice because these principles are right and true for all people everywhere. No nation owns these aspirations, and no nation is exempt from them."

> America must stand firmly for the nonnegotiable demands of human dignity: the rule of law; limits on the absolute power of the state; free speech; freedom of worship; equal justice; respect for women; religious and ethnic tolerance; and respect for private property . . . Embodying lessons from our past and using the opportunity we have today, the national security strategy of the United States must start from these core beliefs and look outward for possibilities to expand liberty.[43]

Nowhere is such an approach more desperately needed, or more attainable, than in Iran. For the Islamic Republic today resembles nothing quite so much as the Soviet Union in the final, dismal days of the Cold War. Clear, unequivocal support of Iran's opposition forces in their resistance to the current regime—and the provision of the needed political backing and economic resources to empower their struggle—could decisively tip the scales in favor of democracy in the Islamic Republic.

The stakes are enormous. Not only would a change of the Iranian system constitute the greatest victory yet in the U.S.-led War on Terror, it would also dovetail with the aspirations of the vast majority of Iranians. In the words of one astute observer of Iranian politics, "[t]he geopolitical interests of the United States coincide with the interests of the majority of Iranians: a fundamental change in the nature of the regime in Tehran. The overthrow of the Islamic Republic of Iran is good for America and good for the Iranian people."[44]

Such a convergence should be a tantalizing possibility for an administration that, in its formative strategy document, has proclaimed its commitment to promoting "a balance of power that favors freedom."

Conclusion:
Promise and Peril

For longtime watchers of Iranian politics, the fall of 2004 brought with it a distinct sense of déjà vu. That November, following months of mounting international concern and growing diplomatic pressure over its atomic ambitions, Iran acquiesced to a new nuclear deal proffered by England, France, and Germany. The preliminary accord grudgingly accepted by Iranian leaders after weeks of public and private wrangling includes a voluntary, temporary suspension of new nuclear construction and enrichment activities, and greater oversight by the International Atomic Energy Agency.[1] In response, officials in Brussels have hailed the start of a potential "new chapter" in ties between Europe and the Islamic Republic,[2] and have moved to revive trade and cooperation talks with Tehran.[3]

And so, the curtain has opened on the latest act in what by now has become a long-running drama. The actors are the same: Europe, bent on diplomatic (and economic) engagement with the Islamic Republic; Iran, shrewdly buying time in order to further its strategic ambitions; and the United States, vacillating between strident rhetoric and political paralysis. The setting is likewise familiar, evoking memories of Iran's broken promises of a nuclear freeze a year earlier and, nine years before that, of the Clinton administration's disastrous "grand bargain" with North Korea: the "Agreed Framework."

Even the denouement is predictable. Already, there are signs that the agreement inked by Iran and the EU has begun to crumble. Iranian officials have taken pains to categorically reject a permanent cessation of uranium enrichment.[4] And, according to Western intelligence reports, not only is Iran still engaged in a vibrant clandestine nuclear trade on the global black market,[5] it has even begun construction of a secret nuclear lab near Isfahan to continue its efforts to enrich uranium out of sight of the European Union.[6]

Yet the November 2004 nuclear pact also constitutes a turning point of sorts—and a clear strategic victory for the regime in Tehran. As a result of the agreement, Iranian officials have succeeded in skillfully separating Europe from the United States on the cardinal issue concerning policy toward Iran—attitudes toward the regime in Tehran itself. For throughout its negotiations with the EU 3, Iran made clear that its chief condition for cooperation was a European pledge to swear off the idea of regime change within the Islamic Republic.[7] Officials in London, Paris, and Berlin, eager to score diplomatic points and defuse international tensions, have signed on the dotted line. In the process, they have shattered any hopes of transnational consensus in dealing with the problem of Iran's nuclear program.

Just as significantly, Tehran has managed, to a large degree, to rob American policy of its momentum. In the wake of the agreement, in a public blow to the United States, the IAEA adopted a softly worded resolution indicating that it would not refer the Iranian "file" to the UN Security Council.[8] The implications of this move have not been lost on Iranian officials. "We have proved that, in an international institution, we are capable of isolating the United States," Hassan Rowhani, the Secretary of Iran's powerful Supreme National Security Council, told a news conference in Tehran in the wake of the IAEA vote. "And that is a great victory."[9]

The United States thus finds itself on the cusp of an international crisis with far-reaching implications. For even if the November 2004 European-Iranian accord proves to be durable, Iran's nuclear program remains only one facet of the broad strategic threat now posed by Tehran to American interests and objectives in the post-9/11 world—one with which Washington can expect little international assistance.

Yet the problem of Iran's atomic advances is enormously significant, because it is intimately related to the progress of freedom in the Islamic Republic. The vast—and growing—domestic opposition visible on the Iranian street today exists precisely because the forces of democracy perceive weaknesses in the current theocratic regime. All of that, however, is likely to change with Iran's acquisition of a nuclear capability. Armed with atomic weaponry, Iran will have far greater ability to repress its domestic opposition with impunity, without concern over decisive international retaliation—much the same way China did in its brutal, bloody suppression of student protests in Tiananmen Square in 1989.

The Middle East stands at a crossroads. More than a quarter century after the Islamic Revolution, Iran has emerged as a cardinal threat to international peace and security. And its nuclear advances, its rising adventurism in the Persian Gulf, Central Asia, and the Caucasus, and its support for the Iraqi insurgency, have put Tehran on a collision course with American policy in the greater Middle East.

Yet Iran should also be the source of great optimism. The groundswell of domestic opposition that is visible on the streets of Iran's cities, in its meeting halls, and on the pages of embattled opposition newspapers, is proof positive of the struggle underway for Iran's soul. It is a contest for power between Iran's anti-Western, corrupt, and authoritarian clerical establishment and the true advocates of Iranian democracy—the Iranian people themselves.

Will Iran, armed with nuclear weapons, emerge to dominate the Middle East? Or will the Islamic Republic give way to a more benign, pro-Western political order?

More and more, it is becoming clear that only the United States can help to answer these questions. With the proper political will, Washington has the ability to contain, deter, and delay Iran's nuclear ambitions, and to empower a post-theocratic transformation within its borders. Just as easily, however, it can once again lapse into inaction, acquiescing to Iranian hegemony in the Persian Gulf, and to the Islamic Republic's increasingly pervasive meddling in Iraq, the Caucasus, and Central Asia.

The choices made by Washington will determine the geopolitical balance of power in the greater Middle East, and the long-term success of American strategy there. And, perhaps more than any other issue, these choices will dictate whether the United States can claim victory on a crucial front in the War on Terror, or if America's vision for the region becomes a victim of Iran's successes.

Notes

Introduction

1. President George W. Bush, State of the Union address, Washington, DC, January 29, 2002, http://frwebgate .access.gpo.gov/cgi-bin/getdoc.cgi?dbname=2002_ presidential_documents&docid=pd04fe02_txt-11.
2. Douglas Jehl, "Iranian Rebels Urge Pentagon Not to Let Iraq Expel Them," *New York Times*, December 19, 2003, 9.
3. Iranian Expediency Council Secretary Mohsen Reza'i, as cited in "Iran to Play Key Role in International Power Politics—Expediency Council Secretary," IRNA (Tehran), March 5, 2003, http://www.profound.com.

Chapter 1

1. Emmanuel Sivan, *Radical Islam: Medieval Theology and Modern Politics* (New Haven: Yale University Press, 1985), 188–207.
2. Preamble of the Constitution of the Islamic Republic of Iran, http://www.oefre.unibe.ch/law/icl/ir00000_.html.
3. Ibid., art. 3, sec. 16 and art. 154.

4. Kenneth Katzman, *The Warriors of Islam: Iran's Revolutionary Guard* (Boulder: Westview Press, 1993), 1–2; Globalsecurity.org, "Pasdaran," http://www .globalsecurity.org/military/world/iran/pasdaran.htm.

5. When necessary, as in the Iran-Iraq War, the *Basij* also served as a reserve pool for the country's two militaries: a devout cadre of ready martyrs. Daniel Byman, Shahram Chubin, Anoushiravan Ehteshami, and Jerrold Green., *Iran's Security Policy in the Post-Revolutionary Era* (Santa Monica: RAND, 2001), 38.

6. Edgar O'Ballance, *Islamic Fundamentalist Terrorism, 1979–95: The Iranian Connection* (New York: New York University Press, 1997), 42.

7. As quoted in Robin Wright, *Sacred Rage: The Wrath of Militant Islam* (New York: Simon & Schuster, 1986), 21.

8. Ibid., 32–35.

9. For more on the roots of the Palestinian revolutionary movement, see Rex Brynen, *Sanctuary and Survival: The PLO in Lebanon* (Boulder: Westview Press, 1990).

10. Magnus Ranstorp, *Hizb'Allah in Lebanon: The Politics of the Western Hostage Crisis* (New York: St. Martin's Press, 1997), 34; Gary C. Gambill and Ziad K. Abednour, "Hezbollah: Between Tehran and Damascus," *Middle East Intelligence Bulletin* 4, no. 2 (2002), http://www.meib.org/articles/0202_11.htm.

11. Rachel Ehrenfeld, *Funding Evil: How Terrorism Is Financed—And How to Stop It* (Chicago: Bonus Books, 2003), 119–20.

12. Ranstorp, *Hizb'Allah in Lebanon*, 34–40.

13. As cited in Center for Special Studies, Intelligence and Terrorism Information Center, "Support for Hezbollah Provided by Iran and Syria, Two Countries Sponsoring Terrorism," June 2003, http://www.intelligence.org .il/eng/bu/hizbullah/chap_c.doc.

14. See, for example, Robert Baer, *See No Evil: The True Story of a Ground Soldier in the CIA's War on Terrorism* (New York: Crown Publishers, 2002).
15. Wright, *Sacred Rage*, 111–21.
16. Byman et al., *Iran's Security Policy in the Post-Revolutionary Era*, 8.
17. Elaine Ganley, "An Iranian Connection Looms over Diplomatic Crisis," Associated Press, August 6, 1986.
18. Jeremy Shapiro and Benedicte Suzan, "The French Experience of Counter-Terrorism," *Survival* 45, no. 1 (2003), 74.
19. National Council of Resistance of Iran, Foreign Affairs Committee, "Dossier: List of Terrorist Acts Abroad," http://www.iranncrfac.org.
20. Amir Taheri, *Holy Terror: Inside the World of Islamic Terrorism* (Bethesda: Adler & Adler, 1987), 112.
21. Taheri, *Holy Terror*, 112.
22. Globalsecurity.org, "Iran-Iraq War (1980–1988)," http://www.globalsecurity.org/military/world/war/iran-iraq.htm.
23. United Nations, Office of the Secretary General, *Report on Iran's Reconstruction Efforts in the Wake of the Conflict between the Islamic Republic of Iran and Iraq*, December 24, 1991, 48.
24. Hooshang Amirahmadi, "Iranian Recovery from Industrial Devastation during War with Iraq," in James K. Mitchell, ed., *The Long Road to Recovery: Community Responses to Industrial Disaster* (Tokyo and New York: United Nations University Press, 1996), http://www.unu.edu/unupress/unupbooks/uu21le/uu21le00.htm#Contents.
25. Robin Wright, *In the Name of God: The Khomeini Decade* (New York: Simon & Schuster, 1990), 209.
26. As cited in Mohammad Mohaddessin, *Islamic Fundamentalism: The New Global Threat* (Washington: Seven Locks Press, 1993), 31.

27. Ibid., 31.
28. Ibid., 36.
29. Ibid., 29–31.
30. As cited in National Council of Resistance of Iran, *Brief on Iran,* no. 1145, May 14, 1999, http://www.iran-e-azad.org/english/boi/11450514_99.html.
31. See, for example, Kenneth R. Timmerman, "Iran's 'Moderates' Are No Reformers," *Brown Journal of World Affairs* 9, issue 2 (2003), 198.
32. "Iran Believed Organizing Global Muslim Terrorism," Associated Press, August 8, 1993.
33. Ely Karmon, "Radical Islamic Political Groups in Turkey," *Middle East Review of International Affairs* 1, no. 4 (1997), http://www.biu.ac.il/Besa/meria/journal/1997/issue4/jv1n4a2.html.
34. A. William Samii, ed., "New Iranian Defector Threatens Relations with Turkey," *Radio Free Europe/Radio Liberty Iran Report* 3, no. 40 (2000).
35. Michael Rubin, "Tactical Terrorism: Iran's Continued Challenge to the Secular Middle East," in Oden Eran and Amnon Cohen, eds., *Israel, the Middle East and Islam: Weighing the Risks and Prospects* (Jerusalem: Hebrew University—Truman Institute, 2003), http://www.washingtoninstitute.org/templateC06.php?CID=620.
36. As cited in Nader Sardari, "Hofer Is Paying for Mykonos Verdict against Iranian Clerics," Iran Press Service, October 11, 1999, http://www.iran-press-service.com/articles/hofer_111099.htm.
37. Elie Rekhess, "The Terrorist Connection—Iran, the Islamic Jihad and Hamas," *Justice* 5 (1995), http://www.mfa.gov.il.
38. "Iran Said Exporting Islamic Revolution via German Mosques," Agence France Presse, March 11, 1995.
39. O'Ballance, *Islamic Fundamentalist Terrorism,* 161–63.

40. U.S. House of Representatives, Committee on International Relations, *Final Report of the Select Committee to Investigate the United States Role in Iranian Arms Transfers to Croatia and Bosnia* (Washington: Government Printing Office, 1996), 167.
41. Daniel Byman and Jerrold Green, *Political Violence and Instability in the Northern Persian Gulf* (Santa Monica: RAND, 1999), 62.
42. Ibid.; "Iranian Terrorism in Bosnia and Croatia," *Iran Brief*, March 3, 1997, http://www.lexis-nexis.com.
43. Mike O'Connor, "Spies for Iranians Are Said to Gain a Hold in Bosnia," *New York Times*, November 28, 1997, 1.
44. Ehrenfeld, *Funding Evil*, 145–48.
45. U.S. Department of State Coordinator for Counterterrorism Phillip Wilcox, Jr., "International Terrorism in Latin America," testimony before the House of Representatives Committee on International Relations, September 28, 1995, http://dosfan.lib.uic.edu/ERC/bureaus/lat/1995/950928WilcoxTerrorism.html.
46. Kenneth R. Timmerman, "New Evidence Fuels Iran Terror Debate," *Insight on the News*, July 7, 2003, 28.
47. Mohamed Osman, "Iran Seeking to Replace Iraq as Sudan's Main Backer," Associated Press, December 14, 1991.
48. Majid Jaber, "Iran's Shadow Looms over Bombings in France," *International Review of Geneva, Switzerland* (Winter 1995–1996), http://www.geocities.com/paris/rue/4637/terr9a.html.
49. See, for example, "Appendix B: Background Information Terrorist Groups," in U.S. Department of State, *Patterns of Global Terrorism, 1996* (April 1997), http://www.state.gov/www/global/terrorism/1996Report/appb.html; Rekhess, "The Terrorist Connection—Iran, the Islamic Jihad and Hamas."

50. Then–CIA Director R. James Woolsey publicly hinted at this linkage in April 1993, when he noted to Congress that Tehran had "applauded" Boudiaf's assassination. R. James Woolsey, statement before the Senate Judiciary Committee, April 21, 1993, http://www.lexis-nexis.com.
51. Andrew Boroweic, "Jihad's Hit List: Egypt, Algeria," *Washington Times*, November 27, 1993, A6.
52. As cited in "Mubarak Blames Iran for Egypt's Violence," United Press International, April 4, 1993.
53. Kenneth Katzman, *Iran: Current Developments and U.S. Policy* (Washington: Congressional Research Service, January 1997), http://www.globalsecurity.org/wmd/library/report/crs/93-033.htm.
54. "Rafsanjani Calls for Stronger Ties with African Countries," Agence France Presse, July 11, 1994.
55. Con Coughlin, "South Africa: Iranian Agents Accused of Training Islamic Terrorists," *Ottawa Citizen*, December 8, 1996.
56. Con Coughlin, "Iran Attempts Islamic Revolution in Africa," *Ottawa Citizen*, March 9, 1997.
57. Dele Olojede, "Militants Mobilizing S. Africa? Hezbollah, Hamas Involvement Seen in Vigilante Campaign," *Newsday* (New York), August 19, 1996.
58. Rekhess, "The Terrorist Connection—Iran, the Islamic Jihad and Hamas."
59. Meir Hatina, *Islam and Salvation in Palestine* (Tel Aviv: Tel Aviv University—Moshe Dayan Center, 2001), 56–57.
60. Rekhess, "The Terrorist Connection—Iran, the Islamic Jihad and Hamas."
61. Brigitte Dusseau, "US Renews Calls for Dialogue with Iran to Address Terrorism Concerns," Agence France Presse, March 11, 1998.
62. Katzman, *Iran: Current Developments and U.S. Policy*.
63. Rekhess, "The Terrorist Connection—Iran, the Islamic Jihad and Hamas."

64. Mohaddessin, *Islamic Fundamentalism*, xxiv.
65. White House, Office of the Press Secretary, "Presidential Address to the Nation," October 7, 2001, http://www.whitehouse.gov/news/releases/2001/10/20011007-8.html.
66. CIA Director George Tenet, "Worldwide Threat—Converging Dangers in a Post 9/11 World," testimony before the Senate Select Committee on Intelligence, February 6, 2002, http://www.cia.gov/cia/public_affairs/speeches/2002/dci_speech_02062002.html.
67. Katzman, *Iran: Current Developments and U.S. Policy.*
68. "Iran Continues to Train Hezbollah," *Middle East Newsline*, April 7, 2002, http://www.menewsline.com/stories/2002/april/04_07_2.html; "Iran Establishes Rocket Training Centers in Lebanon," *Middle East Newsline*, August 8, 2002, http://www.menewsline.com/stories/2002/august/08_08_2.html.
69. Herb Keinon, "Ze'evi: Hizbullah Seeks Chemical Arsenal," *Jerusalem Post*, July 25, 2004, 2.
70. Comments of Labor MK Efraim Sneh, as reported by the Israeli media monitoring group, Independent Media Review and Analysis, January 21, 2004, http://www.imra.org.il.
71. "Hizbullah Suspected of Storing CW," *Middle East Newsline*, May 27, 2002 (author's collection).
72. Richard Chesnoff, "Beware of Unholy Terror Alliance," *New York Daily News*, February 11, 2003, 33.
73. Matthew Levitt, "The Hizballah Threat in Africa," Washington Institute for Near East Policy, *Policywatch* no. 823, January 2, 2004, http://www.washingtoninstitute.org/templateC05.php?CID=1701.
74. Amir Taheri, "An Axis Resurgent," *New York Post*, February 28, 2004, http://www.benadorassociates.com/article/2297.
75. One notable example took place in Europe in the summer of 2002, when Germany's Federal Office for the

Protection of the Constitution went public with news that Hezbollah was actively seeking real estate in Berlin. The planning headquarters, according to news reports, was to serve as the group's leadership hub in Germany and a "training centre" for its supporters in the country, which are estimated at about 800. Some prominent German politicians, like the Christian Democratic Union's Friedbert Pflueger, found the news alarming enough to lobby the government for a national ban on the group. "Hezbollah Planning Berlin Headquarters," *Der Spiegel* (Hamburg), June 24, 2002, http://www.lexis-nexis.com; "Hezbollah Plans to Settle in Berlin," *Die Welt* (Berlin), June 26, 2002, http://www.lexis-nexis.com.

76. See, for example, Isabel Kirshner, "The Changing Colors of Imad Mughniyah," *Jerusalem Report*, March 25, 2002, 25; Dana Priest and Douglas Farah, "Terror Alliance Has U.S. Worried," *Washington Post*, June 30, 2002, A01; Matthew Levitt, *Targeting Terror: U.S. Policy toward Middle Eastern State Sponsors and Terrorist Organizations, Post–September 11* (Washington: Washington Institute for Near East Policy, 2002), 114.

77. In September of 2002, no less senior an official than Deputy Secretary of State Richard Armitage dubbed Hezbollah the premier terrorist threat to international peace and security. "Hezbollah may be the 'A team' of terrorists," Armitage told a Washington conference. "Maybe al-Qaeda is actually the 'B team.'" Richard Armitage, "America's Challenges in a Changed World," remarks to the United States Institute of Peace, Washington, DC, September 5, 2002, http://www.state.gov/s/d/rm/2002/13308.htm.

78. *United States v. Ali Mohamed*, no. S(7) 98 Cr. 1023 (SDNY), October 20, 2000, 28.

79. *The 9/11 Commission Report: Final Report of the National Commission on Terrorist Attacks upon the*

United States (New York: W.W. Norton and Company, 2004), 61.

80. James Risen, "Bin Laden Sought Iran as an Ally, U.S. Intelligence Documents Say," *New York Times*, December 31, 2001, 1.

81. *Corriere Della Serra* (Milan), July 3, 1996, http://www.lexis-nexis.com.

82. Kenneth R. Timmerman, "Iran Cosponsors Al-Qaeda Terrorism," *Insight on the News*, December 3, 2001, 19.

83. Martin Arostegui, "Al-Qaeda Finds a Friend in Iran," *Insight on the News*, November 12, 2002, 39.

84. Dana Milbank, "U.S. Calls on Iran to Stop Sheltering Top Al Qaeda Aides," *Washington Post*, August 29, 2002, A06.

85. Douglas Farah and Dana Priest, "Bin Laden Son Plays Key Role in Al Qaeda," *Washington Post*, October 14, 2003, A01.

86. See, for example, "U.S. Suspects Saudi Bombings Organized by Iran-Based Al-Qaeda Cell," Deutche Presse Agentur, May 18, 2003.

87. "Ansar al-Islam Is Reorganizing Itself in Iran," *Yekgirtu* (Irbil), July 16, 2004, http://tides.carebridge.org/TIRR/DT-IRR260.htm.

88. Rohan Gunaratna, "The Rise of a Networking Terrorist," *The Australian*, July 5, 2004, 14; see also Matthew Levitt, "USA Ties Terrorist Attacks in Iraq to Extensive Zarqawi Network," *Jane's Intelligence Review*, April 1, 2004, http://www.janes.com.

89. Ibid.

90. Ali Nurizadeh, "Iranian Admission of Providing Facilities to Al-Zarqawi in His Terrorist Operations in Iraq," *Al-Sharq al-Awsat* (London), August 11, 2004, http://www.profound.com.

91. Isam al-Amiri, "Al-Zarqawi Does Not Belong to Al-Qa'idah," *Al-Mustaqbal* (Beirut), October 5, 2004, http://www.lexis-nexis.com.

92. Israeli Defense Forces, "Iran and Syria as Strategic Support for Palestinian Terrorism," September 2002, http://www.mfa.gov.il/mfa/mfaarchive/2000_2009/200 2/9/Iran%20and%20Syria%20as%20Strategic%20Su pport%20for%20Palestinia#d.

93. Center for Special Studies, Intelligence and Terrorism Center, "Duplicating the Lebanese Model in the Palestinian Territories: Hezbollah's Support for Palestinian Terrorism," June 2003, http://www.intelli-gence.org.il/eng/bu/hizbullah/hezbollah.htm; Mitchell Ginsburg, "The Reporter: Santorini Arms Ship Completed Three Smuggling Trips before Israel Intercepted It," *Jerusalem Report*, November 18, 2002, 5.

94. Amit Cohen, "The Hezbollah within Us," *Ma'ariv* (Tel Aviv), March 5, 2004, http://www.maarivintl.com/ dev/index.cfm?fuseaction=printArticle&articleID=410 6.

95. Ibid.

96. Amos Harel, "Hezbollah's Terror Factory in the PA," *Ha'aretz* (Tel Aviv), January 11, 2005, http://www .haaretz.com/hasen/spages/525429.html.

97. Ali Nourizadeh, "Islamic Jihad, Hamas and the Palestinian Authority Meet in Iran," *Al-Sharq al-Awsat* (London), June 8, 2002, http://www.profound .com.

98. Matt Rees, "How Hamas-Hezbollah Rivalry Is Terrorizing Israel," *Time*, April 23, 2001, http://www .time.com/time/world/article/0,8599,107347,00.html.

99. Aaron Mannes, "Dangerous Liaisons: Hamas after the Assassination of Yassin," *Middle East Intelligence Bulletin* 6, no. 4 (2004), http://www.meib.org/arti-cles/0404_pal1.htm.

100. "Hamas, Hizbullah Sign Cooperation Accord," *Middle East Newsline*, March 31, 2004, http://www .menewsline.com/stories/2004/march/03_31_1.html.

101. Reuven Paz, "Hamas' Solidarity with Muqtada al-Sadr: Does the Movement Fall under the Control of Hizballah and Iran?" Global Research Center in International Affairs, *PRISM Special Dispatch on Global Jihad,* no. 4/2, August 23, 2004, 4.
102. Levitt, *Targeting Terror*, 64–66, 117–19.
103. "Iran 'Doubling Reward for Suicide Attacks,'" Reuters, July 31, 2003.
104. Mohaddessin, *Islamic Fundamentalism*, 20.
105. Ehud Ya'ari, "Out of Control," *Jerusalem Report*, September 6, 2004, 21.
106. Anton La Guardia, "Iran 'In Control of Terrorism in Israel,'" *Daily Telegraph* (London), October 15, 2004, 14.
107. "Fatah Chief in Iran for Talks," Agence France Presse, December 13, 2004.
108. Interview with Farouk Qaddoumi, *Al-Jazirah* (Doha), December 20, 2004 (author's collection).
109. As cited in Center for Special Studies, Intelligence and Terrorism Information Center, "Hezbollah," July 2003, http://www.intelligence.org.il/eng/bu/hizbullah/pb/app13.htm.
110. Yoav Stern, "Report: Iran Establishes Unit to Recruit Suicide Bombers," *Ha'aretz* (Tel Aviv), May 28, 2004, http://tides.carebridge.org/TIRR/D-TIRR210.htm; "'Iranians Ready for Suicide Raids,'" Reuters, June 6, 2004.
111. Peter Brookes, "Spooks, Lies and Videotape," *New York Post*, July 6, 2004, http://www.heritage.org/Press/Commentary/ed070604a.cfm.
112. As cited in "Iran's Revolutionary Guards Official Threatens Suicide Operations: 'Our Missiles Are Ready to Strike at Anglo-Saxon Culture . . . There Are 29 Sensitive Sites in the U.S. and the West.'" Middle East Media Research Institute, *Special Dispatch No. 73*, May 28, 2004, http://memri.org/bin/articles.cgi?Page=countries&Area=iran&ID=SP72304.

113. "Iran Hosts Leading Insurgency Groups," *Middle East Newsline*, February 1, 2004, http://www.menewsline .com/stories/2004/february/02_01_1.html.

114. As cited in Amir Taheri, "Khomeinists Hammering New Strategy to Oust 'Great Satan,'" *Gulf News*, January 28, 2004, http://www.gulfnews.com/Articles/ opinion.asp?ArticleID=109235.

Chapter 2

1. John J. Lumpkin, "Iran's Nuclear Program Growing at Secret Sites, Rebel Group Alleges," Associated Press, August 14, 2002; "Iran Said to Have Secret Nuclear Facilities," Deutche Press Agentur, August 14, 2002.

2. "Iran's Uranium Programs," *Iran Brief*, June 1, 1995, http://www.lexis-nexis.com.

3. See, for example, Barry Schweid, "Albright Hits Italians over Policies on Libya, Iran, Cuba," Associated Press, February 16, 1997.

4. Anthony Cordesman, *Nuclear Weapons and Iran* (Washington: Center for Strategic and International Studies, 2000), 9, http://www.csis.org/mideast/reports/ irannuclear02072000.PDF.

5. Mohammad Mohaddessin, *Enemies of the Ayatollahs: The Iranian Opposition's War on Islamic Fundamentalism* (London: Zed Books, 2004), 27.

6. Chris Quillen, "Iranian Nuclear Weapons Policy: Past, Present and Possible Future," *Middle East Review of International Affairs* 6, no. 2 (2002), 17.

7. As then-President Ali Khamenei told Iran's Atomic Energy Organization in February 1987, "Regarding atomic energy, we need it now. . . . Our nation has always been threatened from outside. The least we can do to face this danger is to let our enemies know that we can defend ourselves. Therefore, every step you take here is in

defense of your country and your evolution. With this in mind, you should work hard and at great speed." Cited in Henry Sokolski, "The Bomb in Iran's Future," *Middle East Quarterly* 1, no. 2 (1994), http://www.meforum.org/article/222.

8. Cordesman, *Nuclear Weapons and Iran*, 9.

9. Herbert Krosney, *Deadly Business: Legal Deals and Outlaw Weapons* (New York: Four Walls Eight Windows, 1993), 250–51.

10. Author's interview with former Soviet Foreign Ministry official, Palm Beach, Florida, October 28, 2001.

11. Krosney, *Deadly Business*, 250–51.

12. See Charles Fenyvesi, "Russian General Admits: Three More Nukes Are Missing," *U.S. News & World Report* 112, no. 13 (1992), 22; See also Oleg Bukharin and William Potter, "'Potatoes Were Guarded Better': Stealing Nuclear Fuel from the Storage Building at Sevmorput Was—and May Still Be—Easy," *Bulletin of the Atomic Scientists* 51 (1995), 46–51.

13. Rowan Scarborough, "Tale Told of How Iran Nearly Got Nuke Gear," *Washington Times*, November 2, 1996, A3.

14. Rensselaer Lee, "Nuclear Smuggling from the Former Soviet Union: Threats and Responses," Foreign Policy Research Institute *E-Note*, April 27, 2001, http://www.fpri.org/enotes/russia.20010427.lee.nuclearsmuggling.html.

15. Brenda Shaffer, *Partners in Need: The Strategic Relationship of Russia and Iran* (Washington: Washington Institute for Near East Policy, 2001), 11–12, 71.

16. Ibid.

17. *Priroda* (Moscow), August 1995, as cited in Shaffer, *Partners in Need*, 65.

18. Assistant Secretary of State for Nonproliferation Robert J. Einhorn, testimony before the Senate Foreign

Relations Committee, October 5, 2000, http://www
.state.gov/www/policy_remarks/2000/001005_ein-
horn_sfrc.html.

19. "China Sells Reactor to Iran," *Middle East Defense News 5*, no. 23, September 14, 1992, http://www.lexis-nexis.com.

20. Office of the Secretary of Defense, *Proliferation: Threat and Response, 1996* (Washington: U.S. Department of Defense, 1996), 14.

21. "US Gets China to Limit Nuclear Aid, Arms Sales to Iran: Report," Agence France Presse, October 24, 1997.

22. Barton Gellman and John Pomfret, "U.S. Action Stymied China Sale to Iran," *Washington Post,* March 13, 1998, A1.

23. Bill Gertz, "China Still Shipping Arms Despite Pledges," *Washington Times*, April 15, 1999, A1.

24. "Secret Nuclear Sites Detailed," *Iran Brief*, November 6, 1995, http://www.lexis-nexis.com.

25. Ibid.

26. John Hughes, "Arms Buildup Belies the Image of a 'Moderate' Regime," *Christian Science Monitor*, February 6, 1992, 19.

27. David E. Sanger, "Pakistan Found to Aid Iran Nuclear Efforts," *New York Times*, September 2, 2004, 12; James Traub, "The Netherworld of Proliferation," *New York Times Magazine*, June 1, 2004, 49; Bronwen Maddox, "Iran Admits Pakistan Gave Key Nuclear Help," *Times* (London), November 13, 2003.

28. Mohaddessin, *Enemies of the Ayatollahs*, 38-39; Marshall Breit, *Fact Sheet: Iran's Programs to Produce Plutonium and Highly Enriched Uranium*, Carnegie Endowment for International Peace, April 1, 2004, http://www.ceip.org/files/projects/npp/resources/Factshe ets/iransnuclearprogram.htm.

29. Globalsecurity.org, "Arak," http://www.globalsecurity .org/wmd/world/iran/arak.htm; Breit, *Fact Sheet: Iran's*

Programs to Produce Plutonium and Highly Enriched Uranium.

30. "Russia Has Finished Construction Work at Bushehr Nuclear Reactor," Associated Press, October 15, 2004.

31. Globalsecurity.org, "Esfahan," http://www.globalsecurity.org/wmd/world/iran/esfahan.htm; "Iran Reveals Uranium, But Pledges Peaceful Use." *Sydney Morning Herald*, February 11, 2003, http://www.smh.com.au/articles/2003/02/10/1044725733294.html?oneclick =true.

32. Michael Rubin, "Iran's Burgeoning WMD Programs," *Middle East Intelligence Bulletin* 4, no. 3 (2002), http://www.meib.org/articles/0203_irn1.htm; Globalsecurity.org, "Kaleye Electric Company," http://www.globalsecurity.org/wmd/world/iran/tehran-kalaye.htm; Mohaddessin, *Enemies of the Ayatollahs*, 30.

33. Douglas Jehl, "Group Says Iran Has Secret Nuclear Arms Program," *New York Times*, November 17, 2004, 4; "Iranian Group Claims 'New' Nuke Facility in Tehran," *CNN*, November 17, 2004, http://www.cnn.com/2004/WORLD/meast/11/17/iran.nuclear/index.html.

34. Jon Boyle, "Iran Using Lasers to Enrich Uranium—Exile Group," Reuters, November 19, 2004.

35. Globalsecurity.org, "Saghand," http://www.globalsecurity.org/wmd/world/iran/saghand.htm.

36. "Iran Plans to Exploit Uranium," *Radio Free Europe/ Radio Liberty Newsline* 7, no. 26 (2003).

37. Robin Gedye, "Iran's Nuclear History," *Daily Telegraph* (London), September 10, 2003, http://www.telegraph.co.uk/news/main.jhtml?xml=/news/2003/09/10/wiran210.xml&sSheet=/news/2003/09/10/ixnewstop.html.

38. Ali Akbar Dareini, "Iran to Inaugurate Uranium Ore Plant," Associated Press, January 24, 2005.

39. "IAEA Official Says Iran Must Explain Discovery of Uranium," ISNA (Tehran), February 28, 2004, http://www.lexis-nexis.com.
40. Kenneth R. Timmerman, "Iran's Nuclear Program: Myth and Reality," paper presented before the USPID Sixth International Castglioncello Conference, Castglioncello, Italy, September 30, 1995, http://www.uspid.dsi.unimi.it/proceed/cast95/ItalyIran.html.
41. "Russia to Give Iran More Nuclear Reactors: Report," Agence France Presse, August 27, 1995.
42. Federation of American Scientists, "Chalus," http://www.fas.org/nuke/guide/iran/facility/chalus.htm.
43. Maxim Kniazkov, "Iran Seen as Middle East Nuclear Threat," *Voice of America*, December 27, 1996, http://www.profound.com; Globalsecurity.org, "Darkhovin," http://www.globalsecurity.org/wmd/world/iran/darkhovin.htm.
44. "Secret Nuclear Sites Detailed," *Iran Brief*, November 6, 1995, http://www.lexis-nexis.com.
45. Ibid.
46. Federation of American Scientists, "Fasa," http://www.fas.org/nuke/guide/iran/facility/fasa.htm; Kenneth R. Timmerman, "Tehran's A-Bomb Program Shows Startling Progress," *Washington Times*, May 8, 1995, A1.
47. "China Helps Iran Enrich Its Uranium: Report," Agence France Presse, September 25, 1995.
48. Iranian Member of Parliament Ahmad Shirzad, November 24, 2003, remarks before legislative session, as cited in *Radio Free Europe/Radio Liberty Iran Report* 6, no. 47 (2003).
49. See, for example, Karim Sajidpour, "Iranians Don't Want to Go Nuclear," *Washington Post*, February 3, 2004, A19.
50. Reuters, April 19, 2003, as cited in Ray Takeyh, "Iran's Nuclear Calculations," *World Policy Journal* 20, no. 2 (2003), 23.

51. Despite solemn pledges that the reactors built by the Korean Energy Development Organization (KEDO) were proliferation resistant, critics saw this as a particularly ominous move; in principle, and subsequently at times even in practice, the United States had acquiesced to a nuclear North Korea.

52. See, for example, Nicholas Eberstadt, "North Korea: Beyond Appeasement," in Robert Kagan and William Kristol, eds., *Present Dangers: Crisis and Opportunity in American Foreign and Defense Policy* (San Francisco: Encounter Books, 2000), 145–75.

53. Louis Charbonneau, "Iran Wants No 'Regime Change' Guarantee," Reuters, October 15, 2004.

54. "Iranian Foreign Minister Holds Talks with Visiting North Korean Official," IRNA (Tehran), December 14, 2003, http://www.profound.com.

55. As cited in Karl Vick, "Iranians Assert Right to Nuclear Weapons," *Washington Post*, March 11, 2003, A16.

56. David Rennie, "Alarm as Iran Takes Another Step Towards Nuclear Weapons," *Daily Telegraph* (London), March 10, 2003, 12.

57. International Atomic Energy Agency, Report by the Director General, *Implementation of the NPT Safeguards Agreement in the Islamic Republic of Iran*, June 6, 2003, http://globalsecurity.org/wmd/library/report/2003/gov2003-40.pdf.

58. "IAEA Resolution on Iran's Nuclear Program," Agence France Presse, November 26, 2003.

59. Stephen Fidler, "Iran Centrifuge Plan Dashes Hopes of a Nuclear Deal," *Financial Times* (London), June 25, 2004, http://www.profound.com.

60. Con Coughlin, "Five N-Bombs within Iran's Grasp as West Prevaricates," *Sunday Telegraph* (London), September 12, 2004, 29.

61. Author's conversations with U.S. government officials, Washington, DC, June and July 2004.

62. See, for example, "Weighing the Options: U.S. Faces Closing Window of Opportunity to Stop Iran's Nukes," *Geostrategy-Direct*, September 28, 2004, http://www .geostrategy-direct.com/geostrategy-direct/secure/ 2004/9_28/do.asp.

63. David Ratner, "Ze'evi: Iran Will Be Able to Enrich Uranium in 6 Months," *Ha'aretz* (Tel Aviv), January 12, 2005, http://www.haaretz.com/hasen/spages/525989 .html.

64. Ibid.

65. In fact, Russia's Foreign Ministry has publicly signaled that it will oppose any attempt to refer Iran to the United Nations Security Council for its nuclear activities. "Moscow: Iran's Nuclear File Shall Not Go to UN Security Council," RIA-Novosti (Moscow), November 16, 2004, http://en.rian.ru/rian/index.cfm?prd_id= 160&msg_id=5094904&startrow=1&date=2004-11-16&do_alert=0.

66. Cited in "Middle East Reverberations of the Nuclear Tests in India and Pakistan," Washington Institute for Near East Policy, *Policywatch* no. 322, June 19, 1998, http://www.washingtoninstitute.org/templateC05.php? CID=1200.

67. Ibid.

68. "Senior Iranian Official Welcomes Pakistani Nuclear Tests," Agence France Presse, June 5, 1998.

69. Ibid.

70. Bin Laden's communiqué was cited in the indictment of Zacarias Moussaoui, the suspected twentieth September 11th hijacker, that was handed down by the U.S. District Court for the Eastern District of Virginia in December 2001. The indictment can be accessed online at http://www.usdoj.gov/ag/moussaouiindictment.htm.

71. See, for example, Michael Eisenstadt, "Iran under Khatami: Weapons of Mass Destruction, Terrorism, and the Arab-Israeli Conflict," testimony before the Senate

Foreign Relations Committee Subcommittee on Near East and South Asian Affairs, May 14, 1998, http://www.iranwatch.org/government/US/Congress/Hearings/sfrc-051498/us-sfrc-eisenstadt-051498.htm; Mohaddessin, *Enemies of the Ayatollahs*, 26-31; Mohammad Mohaddessin, *Islamic Fundamentalism: The New Global Threat* (Washington: Seven Locks Press, 1993), 131–39.

72. For example, following the summer 2003 test of the *Shahab-3*, the Iranian regime publicly announced that it had inducted the advanced medium-range missile into the *Pasdaran*. See "Iranian Leader Oversees Handover of Shahab-3 Missile to Revolutionary Guard," *Vision of the Islamic Republic of Iran Network 1* (Tehran), July 20, 2003, http://www.lexis-nexis.com.

73. "Iran Establishes Rocket Training Centers in Lebanon," *Middle East Newsline*, August 8, 2002, http://www.menewsline.com/stories/2002/august/08_08_2.html.

74. "Hezbollah Amassing Weapons in Southern Lebanon," *Aerospace and Defense*, September 30, 2002, http://www.profound.com; Michael R. Gordon, "Hezbollah's Rocket Arsenal Worries Officials," *Edmonton Journal* (Alberta), September 27, 2002, B9.

75. Uzi Mahnaimi, "Iranian Missiles Can Reach Israel," *Sunday Times* (London), October 20, 2002, 22.

76. "Report: N. Korea Sold Missiles to Mideast," United Press International, October 28, 2003.

77. Defense Intelligence Agency Director Thomas R. Wilson, "Global Threats and Challenges," testimony before the Senate Armed Services Committee, March 19, 2002, http://armed-services.senate.gov/statemnt/2002/March/Wilson.pdf.

78. Assistant Secretary of State for Intelligence and Research Carl W. Ford, Jr., "Reducing the Threat of Chemical and Biological Weapons," testimony before the Senate Committee on Foreign Relations, March 19, 2002,

http://frwebgate.access.gpo.gov/cgi-in/getdoc.cgi?
dbname=107_senate_hearings&docid=f:79961.wais.

79. Walid Abi-Murshid and Ali Nurizadeh, "Iranian-Libyan
    Military Cooperation Plan Frozen Because of Differences
    over al-Sadr," *Al-Sharq al-Awsat* (London), February
    25, 2002, as cited in Rubin, "Iran's Burgeoning WMD
    Programs."

80. "Report: Libya Goes Ballistic in $13.5 Billion Deal with
    Iran," *worldtribune.com*, August 21, 2002, http://216
    .26.163.62/2002/me_libya_08_21.html.

81. Con Coughlin, "Iran Poised for Terror Campaign
    against Gaddafi," *Daily Telegraph* (London), February
    29, 2004, 29.

82. Herb Keinon, "Ze'evi: Hizbullah Seeks Chemical
    Arsenal," *Jerusalem Post*, July 25, 2004, 2.

83. See, for example, Alexander Rose, "Syria Upgrading
    Scud-C Missiles," *National Post* (Toronto), July 2,
    2002, A10.

84. "Report: Syria Has 100 Nerve-Gas Missiles Aimed at
    Israel," *Ha'aretz* (Tel Aviv), July 31, 2003, http://www
    .haaretz.com/hasen/spages/324288.html.

85. As cited in David E. Sanger, "Bush Says U.S. Will Not
    Tolerate Building of Nuclear Arms by Iran," *New York
    Times*, June 19, 2003, 1.

86. Arnaud de Borchgrave, "Pakistan, Saudi Arabia in
    Secret Nuke Pact," *Washington Times*, October 22,
    2003, A01.

87. Patrick Clawson, *Nuclear Proliferation in the Middle
    East: Who's Next after Iran?* (Washington: Nonprolif-
    eration Policy Education Center, 2003), http://www
    .npec-web.org/projects/clawson.pdf.

88. "'Traces of Plutonium Found near Facility,'" *Jordan
    Times* (Amman), November 7, 2004, http://www.jor-
    dantimes.com/sun/news/news5.htm.

89. Clawson, *Nuclear Proliferation in the Middle East:
    Who's Next after Iran?*

NOTES

90. Defense Intelligence Agency Director Lowell E. Jacoby, "Current and Projected National Security Threats to the United States," statement before the U.S. Senate Select Committee on Intelligence, February 24, 2004, http://intelligence.senate.gov/0402hrg/040224/jacoby.pdf.
91. *Draft Report: Restraining a Nuclear-Ready Iran: Seven Levers* (Washington: Nonproliferation Policy Education Center, September 13, 2004), http://www.npec-web.org/projects/Iran/2004-09-13SevenLevers.pdf.

Chapter 3

1. Defense Intelligence Agency Director Thomas R. Wilson, "Global Threats and Challenges," statement before the Senate Armed Services Committee, March 19, 2002, http://www.senate.gov/~armed_services/statemnt/2002/March/Wilson.pdf.
2. Michael Eisenstadt, "The Military Dimension," in Patrick Clawson et al., *Iran under Khatami: A Political, Economic and Military Assessment* (Washington: Washington Institute for Near East Policy, 1998), 74-78.
3. U.S. Department of Energy, Energy Information Administration, "Crude Oil Prices, Selected Crudes and World Average," http://tonto.eia.doe.gov/oog/ftparea/wogirs/xls/psw13.xls#'3-Weekly World and U.S.'!A1.
4. "Iran," *Economist Intelligence Unit*, March 2002, 5.
5. Michael Rubin, "What Are Iran's Domestic Priorities?" *Middle East Review of International Affairs* 6, no. 2 (2002), 26–27.
6. Alexei Germanovich, "Armaments for the Ayatollahs," *Vedemosti* (Moscow), March 12, 2001, http://www.lexis-nexis.com.
7. See Ayalet Savyon, "Iran's Armament—A Central Element in Establishing Itself as a Regional Superpower," Middle East Media Research Institute, *Inquiry and*

Analysis, no. 89, March 26, 2002, http://memri.org/bin/articles.cgi?Page=countries&Area=iran&ID=IA8902.

8. Vladimir Isachenkov, "Iran, Russia Defy U.S. with Pact," Associated Press, March 12, 2001.

9. Alice Lagando, "Moscow Defies US with Iran Arms Deals," *Times* (London), March 13, 2001, http://www.lexis-nexis.com; Ivan Safronov, "Iran Asks for Weapons," *Kommersant* (Moscow), March 15, 2001, http://www.lexis-nexis.com; "Iran Planning to Buy Russian SAM Systems," Itar-TASS (Moscow), March 19, 2001, http://www.lexis-nexis.com.

10. "Iranian Defense Minister in Moscow for Arms Talks," *Radio Free Europe/Radio Liberty Newsline* 5, no. 186 (2001).

11. Victor Yasmann, ed., "Kremlin Adviser Explains Putin's Decision to Ally with West," *Radio Free Europe/Radio Liberty Security Watch* 2, no. 39 (2001).

12. "Russia Firms Accord with Iran," *Jane's Defence Weekly*, October 5, 2001, http://www.janes.com.

13. Richard F. Grimmett, *Conventional Arms Transfers to Developing Nations, 1993–2000* (Washington: Congressional Research Service, August 2001), 28.

14. Malik, J. Mohan, "China and the Nuclear Non-Proliferation Regime," *Contemporary Southeast Asia* 22, no. 3 (2000), 445–78; "China Reported to Be Improving Iran's FL-10," *Jane's Missiles & Rockets*, September 1, 1999, http://www.janes.com; Bill Gertz, "China Agrees to Deal with Iran on Missiles," *Washington Times*, August 19, 1999, A1.

15. "New Iranian Weapons," *Iran Brief*, March 4, 1996, http://www.lexis-nexis.com.

16. Based on figures provided in Michael Eisenstadt's *Iranian Military Power: Capabilities and Intentions* (Washington: Washington Institute for Near East Policy, 1996), and Anthony Cordesman's *The Arab-Israeli*

Military Balance in 2002 (Washington: Center for Strategic and International Studies, 2002).

17. Defense Intelligence Agency Director Lowell E. Jacoby, "Current and Projected National Security Threats to the United States," statement before the Senate Select Committee on Intelligence, February 11, 2003, http://intelligence.senate.gov/0402hrg/040224/jacoby.pdf.

18. Central Intelligence Agency Director George J. Tenet, "Current and Projected National Security Threats," statement before the Senate Armed Services Committee, February 2, 1999, http://www.cia.gov/cia/public_affairs/speeches/1999/ddci_testimony_022499.html.

19. Michael Eisenstadt, "Iran—Capabilities and Intentions," in *Missile Defenses and American Security, 2002: A New Era* (Lanham, MD: University Press of America—American Foreign Policy Council, 2004), 31–32.

20. U.S. Central Intelligence Agency, *Unclassified Report to Congress on the Acquisition of Technology Relating to Weapons of Mass Destruction and Advanced Conventional Munitions, 1 July–30 December 2003*, November 2004, http://www.cia.gov/cia/reports/721_reports/july_dec2003.htm#iran.

21. Ibid.; see also Uzi Mahnaimi, "Iranian Missiles Can Reach Israel," *Sunday Times* (London), October 20, 2002, http://www.lexis-nexis.com.

22. "Iran Says It Has Missile with 1,250-Mile Range," Reuters, October 5, 2004.

23. See, for example, "Iran Begins Serial Production of Shahab-3," *Jane's Defence Weekly*, October 10, 2001, http://www.janes.com.

24. "Iran Conducts Testing of Taepo Dong," *Middle East Newsline*, October 25, 2002, http://www.iranvajahan.net/cgi-bin/news_en.pl?l=en&y=2002&m=12&d=05&a=2.

25. "Iran Could Test ICBMs as Early as 2005," *Middle East Newsline*, May 20, 2004, http://www.menewsline.com/stories/2004/may/05_20_1.html.

26. Mohammad Mohaddessin, *Islamic Fundamentalism: The New Global Threat* (Washington: Seven Locks Press, 1993), 131–39.

27. See, for example, "CW Deliveries from China," *Iran Brief*, July 6, 1995, http://www.lexis-nexis.com.

28. Eisenstadt, *Iranian Military Power*, 26.

29. DCI Nonproliferation Center Deputy Director A. Norman Schindler, "Iran's Weapons of Mass Destruction Programs," statement before the Senate Governmental Affairs Committee International Security, Proliferation and Federal Services Subcommittee, September 21, 2000, http://www.cia.gov/cia/public_affairs/speeches/2000/schindler_WMD_092200.htm.

30. Amir Oren, "Mossad Chief: Israel Must Foil Regional Nuclear Arms Plans," *Ha'aretz* (Tel Aviv), June 27, 2002, http://www.haaretzdaily.com/hasen/pages/ShArt.jhtml?itemNo=180835&contrassID=1&subContrassID=0&sbSubContrassID=0.

31. Schindler, "Iran's Weapons of Mass Destruction Programs."

32. "Iranian Dissident Group Claims Tehran Has Biological Weapons," Agence France Presse, May 15, 2003.

33. National Council of Resistance of Iran, "Iranian Regime's Programs for Biological and Microbial Weapons," Washington, DC, May 15, 2003, http://www.globalsecurity.org/wmd/library/news/iran/2003/iran-030515-bw.htm.

34. See, for example, "Report: Libya Goes Ballistic in $13.5 Billion Deal with Iran," worldtribune.com, August 21, 2002, http://216.26.163.62/2002/me_libya_08_21.html.

35. See, for example, Alexander Rose, "Syria Upgrading Scud-C Missiles," *National Post* (Toronto), July 2, 2002, A10.

36. *Vision of the Islamic Republic of Iran Network 1*, Tehran, April 10, 2000, http://www.lexis-nexis.com.

37. "Iran, Kuwait Sign Agreement on Military Cooperation," Xinhua News Agency, October 2, 2002, http://www.profound.com; "Iran, Kuwait Sign Military Agreement," Associated Press, October 2, 2002.

38. Ali Akbar Dareini, "Iran, Saudi Arabia Sign Landmark Security Pact," Associated Press, April 17, 2001.

39. See, for example, Iranian Foreign Minister Kamal Kharrazi's January 7, 2001, address to the Annual Persian Gulf International Seminar, as reproduced in *Ettela'at* (Tehran), January 13, 2001, http://www.lexis-nexis.com.

40. Cited on *Fox News*, September 18, 2001, http://www.foxnews.com/story/0,2933,34552,00.html.

41. See, for example, John Daniszewski, "Taliban Attack on Border Post Repelled, Iran Claims," *Los Angeles Times*, October 9, 1998, 13; Kamal Kharrazi, "Iran and Afghanistan," *Perceptions* 7, no. 1 (2002), http://www.mfa.gov.tr/grupa/percept/VII-1/kamal.kharrazi.htm.

42. A. William Samii, ed., "Tehran Continues Afghan 'Psyops,'" *Radio Free Europe/Radio Liberty Iran Report* 5, no. 3 (2002); A. William Samii, ed., "President Bush Speaks on Radio Farda," *Radio Free Europe/Radio Liberty Iran Report* 5, no. 47 (2002).

43. A. William Samii, ed., "Iran Uses 'Black Propaganda' in Afghanistan," *Radio Free Europe/Radio Liberty Iran Report* 5, no. 5 (2002).

44. Samii, "Tehran Continues Afghan 'Psyops.'"

45. Peter Baker, "Warlord Gets Money, Arms from Iran, Afghan Aides Say," *Washington Post*, February 7, 2002, A9.

46. A. William Samii, ed., "Aghajari Death Sentence Still in Place," *Radio Free Europe/Radio Liberty Iran Report* 6, no. 4 (2003).

47. A. William Samii, ed., "President Bush Speaks on Radio Farda," *Radio Free Europe/Radio Liberty Iran Report* 5, no. 5 (2002).

48. Mohammad Mohaddessin, *Enemies of the Ayatollahs: The Iranian Opposition's War on Islamic Fundamentalism* (London: Zed Books, 2004), 28.

49. *Saisat-e Rouz* (Tehran), February 18, 2003, as translated in "Iranian Defense Minister on Iran's Defense Doctrine," Middle East Media Research Institute, *Special Dispatch* no. 502, May 9, 2003, http://memri.org/bin/articles.cgi? Page=countries&Area=iran&ID=SP50203.

50. Mohaddessin, *Enemies of the Ayatollahs*, 28.

51. For more, see the author's "The New Battleground: Central Asia and the Caucasus," *The Washington Quarterly* 28, no. 1 (2004/2005), 59–69.

52. "Russia, EU Oppose Inclusion of Iran on 'Axis of Evil' List," *Tehran Times*, July 21, 2002, http://www.tehran times.com/archives/Description.asp?Da=7/22/02&Cat= 4&Num=004.

53. "Russia to Start Assembling Iran Reactor by Year's End," Itar-TASS (Moscow), November 16, 2001, http://www .profound.com; "Russian Nuke Reactor Leaves for Iran," *Middle East Newsline*, November 18, 2001, http://www .menewsline.com/stories/2001/november/11_19_1.html.

54. Nick Paton Walsh, "Russia Defies US with Plan to Build More Nuclear Reactors in Iran," *Guardian* (London), July 27, 2002, 19.

55. "Russia Has Finished Construction Work at Bushehr Nuclear Reactor," Associated Press, October 15, 2004.

56. See, for example, Philip Sherwell, "Russia Adds Range to Iran's Latest Missiles," *Daily Telegraph* (London), November 10, 2002, 29.

57. Uzi Rubin, "Iran's New Shihab Missile and the Russian Connection," *Middle East Missiles Monitor*, September 24, 2004, http://www.me-monitor.com/docframes.asp? file=files/shihab_ss4.htm.

58. "Khatami in Beijing to Seal Iran's 'Strategic Partnership' with China," *Mideast Mirror* 14, no. 118 (2000), http://www.lexis-nexis.com.

59. "Evaluation of President's Trip to China," *Abrar* (Tehran), June 29, 2000, http://wnc.fedworld.gov.

60. See, for example, "Iranian Commander Visiting China to Boost Ties," IRNA (Tehran), October 10, 2003, http://www.lexis-nexis.com.

61. "N. Korea Lines Up Arms Deal," *Daily Telegraph* (Sydney), August 7, 2003, 31.

62. "The Tehran-Pyongyang Axis," *Washington Times,* August 8, 2003, A18.

63. "Lebanese President Says Iran and Lebanon 'Strategic Allies,'" IRNA (Tehran), February 28, 2004, http://www.lexis-nexis.com.

64. M. Javad Zarif, "A Neighbor's Vision of the New Iraq," *New York Times*, May 10, 2003, 21.

65. "Iran: Foreign Minister Calls for Joint Persian Gulf Security System," IRNA (Tehran), February 14, 2004, http://www.lexis-nexis.com.

66. "Iran: Def Min Shamkhani Stresses Expansion of Iran-Syria Defense Cooperation," IRNA (Tehran), February 26, 2004, http://www.lexis-nexis.com.

67. "Defence Minister Says Syria a Part of Iran's Security," IRNA (Tehran), February 26, 2004, http://www.lexisnexis.com.

68. "Syria Part of Iran's Security: Shamkhani," *Tehran Times*, February 28, 2004, http://www.profound.com.

69. Jackie Hogi, "Iran Pledges to Back Syria If Israel Attacks," *Ma'ariv* (Tel Aviv), February 29, 2004, http://www.maarivintl.com/index.cfm?fuseaction=article&articleID=3770.

70. "Lebanese President Says Iran and Lebanon 'Strategic Allies,'" IRNA (Tehran), February 28, 2004, http://www.lexis-nexis.com.

71. Richard Waddington, "Egypt, Iran Agree for Joint Efforts on World Problems," Reuters, December 11, 2003; "Egypt, Iran Prepare for Reconciliation," *Middle East Newsline*, December 12, 2003, http://www.menewsline.com/stories/2003/december/12_12_4.html.

72. "Tehran City Council Approves Renaming Controversial Street," IRNA (Tehran), January 6, 2004, http://www.lexis-nexis.com; Greg LaMotte, "Egypt-Iran Relations Reach New High with Mubarak's Planned Visit to Tehran," *VOA News*, January 6, 2004, http://www.profound.com.

73. Umit Enginsoy and Burak Ege Bekdil, "Turkey-Iran Pact Irks United States," *Defense News*, August 9, 2004, 6; See also Bulent Aydemir, "'We Will Do Whatever Is Necessary,'" *Sabah* (Istanbul), July 29, 2004, http://www.profound.com.

74. "Iran Has Signed Security Agreement with Persian Gulf Countries—Deputy Minister," Fars News Agency (Tehran), June 20, 2004, http://www.profound.com.

75. Mehdi Shakiba'i, "The Persian Gulf and the West's New Security Approach toward the Middle East," *E'Temad* (Tehran), October 21, 2004, http://www.lexis-nexis.com.

76. Defense Intelligence Agency Director Lowell E. Jacoby, "Current and Projected National Security Threats to the United States," statement before the Senate Select Committee on Intelligence, February 24, 2004, http://intelligence.senate.gov/0402hrg/040224/jacoby.pdf.

77. These include "the design and production of long-range surface-to-surface Shahab-3 missiles; production of different varieties of surface-to-surface and air-to-surface missiles, long-range shore-sea missiles, surface-to-air missiles and all types of guided bombs and missiles for fighter aircraft; design and production of different types of vessels and modern radars; manufacture of T-72, Chieftain, M-60, M-47 and Scorpion tanks; production

of armored and amphibious BTR-82 and M-113 personnel carriers; design and production of missile engines using compound solid fuel; design and renovation of different military and non-military helicopters; overhaul of military and passenger planes' engines; manufacture of supersonic Simorgh training aircraft and different types of unmanned air vehicles for reconnaissance; production of Iran-140 passenger plane; design and production of national Khaybar arms as reported; production of recoil guns with different calibre and different types of Katiyusha and air defence guns; and production of other kinds of arms and ammunitions for the Armed Forces." *Vision of the Islamic Republic of Iran Network 1* (Tehran), September 27, 2003, http://www.lexis-nexis.com.

78. "Iran Is Gathering Troops on Border with Azerbaijan," *Uch Nogta* (Baku), October 22, 2003 (author's collection); "'Lightning' Fighter Jet to Join Iran's Air Force Soon," Mehr News Agency, (Tehran), April 14, 2004, http://www.profound.com.

79. ISNA (Tehran), November 2, 2004, http://www.profound.com.

80. "Iran Deploys Ballistic Missile from Sea Vessel," *Middle East Newsline*, October 14, 2004 (author's collection).

81. "Iran Confiscated Three British Warships," Associated Press, June 21, 2004; Scott Peterson, British Sailors Are Latest Pawns in Iranian Politics," *Christian Science Monitor*, June 24, 2004, 07.

82. Ali Nourizadeh, "Source: Real Reason for Seizure of Boats Was Revolutionary Guards' Desire to Release Detainees Held by the British Forces," *Al-Sharq al-Awsat* (London), June 23, 2004, http://www.profound.com.

83. Michael Ledeen, "Ready for $60-a-Barrel Oil?" *National Review Online*, June 22, 2004. http://www.nationalreview.com/ledeen/ledeen200406220842.asp.

84. Cited in Adrian Blomfield, "Iraq Issues Threat to Iran over Insurgents," *Daily Telegraph* (London), July 21, 2004, 13.
85. Mohaddessin, *Enemies of the Ayatollahs*, 152–56.
86. Edward T. Pound, "Special Report: The Iran Connection," *U.S. News & World Report* 137, no. 18, (2004), 34.
87. "Iran's Role in the Recent Uprising in Iraq," Middle East Media Research Institute, *Special Dispatch* no. 692, April 9, 2004, http://www.memri.org/bin/articles.cgi?Page=countries&Area=iran&ID=SP69204.
88. *Al-Sharq Al-Awsat* (London), July 20, 2004, as cited in "Iraqi Defense and Interior Ministers Accuse Iran of Terrorism against Iraq, Threaten Retaliation within Iran," Middle East Media Research Institute, *Special Dispatch* no. 750, July 20, 2004, http://www.memri.org/bin/articles.cgi?Page=countries&Area=iran&ID=SP75004.
89. See, for example, "Iranian Drug Dealers Disguise as Clerics to Sell Narcotics in Iraq," *Al-Hayat* (London), November 28, 2003, http://www.lexis-nexis.com.
90. See, for example, Louis Meixler, "Extremists Moving across Iran-Iraq Border," Associated Press, November 8, 2004.
91. "Al-Zarqawi and elements of his organization's command (*Ansar al-Islam*) do not need prior authority to enter Iran," Brigadier General Qasem Solaimani, the commander of the *Pasdaran*'s Qods Corps, revealed to a seminar at Tehran's Imam Hoseyn University in August 2004. "There are certain border points from Halabjah in the north to Ilam in the south. Al-Zarqawi and more than 20 fighters from *Ansar al-Islam*... can enter the Iranian territories through them whenever they want." Ali Nurizadeh, "Iranian Admission of Providing Facilities to Al-Zarqawi in His Terrorist Operations in Iraq," *Al-Sharq al-Awsat* (London), August 11, 2004, http://www.profound.com.

92. A. William Samii, ed., "Exile Claims Iran Involved in al-Hakim Assassination," *Radio Free Europe/Radio Liberty Iran Report* 6, no. 44 (2003).

93. "Abdul Majid Al-Khoei," *Times* (London), April 11, 2003, 40.

94. Niles Lathem and Uri Dan, "Iran, Hezbollah Aid Crazed Cleric," *New York Post*, April 11, 2004, 4; see also A. William Samii, ed., "Tehran Debates SCIRI's Role in Iraq," *Radio Free Europe/Radio Liberty Iran Report* 6, no. 41 (2003).

95. Pound, "Special Report: The Iran Connection."

96. "Iran Financing in Iraq Uncovered," *Geostrategy-Direct*, November 2, 2004, http://www.geostrategydirect.com/geostrategy-direct/secure/2004/11_02/ba.asp?.

97. Kathleen Ridolfo, "The Post-Hussein Media Environment in Iraq," *Radio Free Europe/Radio Liberty Iraq Report* 6, no. 49 (2003).

98. "Iran's Role in the Recent Uprising in Iraq," Middle East Media Research Institute, *Special Dispatch* no. 692, April 9, 2004, http://www.memri.org/bin/articles.cgi?Page=countries&Area=iran&ID=SP69204.

99. Pound, "Special Report: The Iran Connection."

100. "Iran's Role in the Recent Uprising in Iraq."

101. Pound, "Special Report: The Iran Connection."

102. Ali Nurizadeh, "Iranian Source: Revolution Guard Trains 1,000 Muqtada al-Sadr Supporters on Guerilla Warfare, Explosions," *Al-Sharq al-Awsat* (London), April 9, 2004, http://www.profound.com.

103. Lou Marano, "Iraqi: Hamas, Hezbollah Operating in Iraq," United Press International, January 15, 2004; See also Sharon Behn, "Hezbollah, Hamas Office Reported in Iraq," *Washington Times*, March 31, 2004, A19.

104. Raymond Tanter, "Iran's Threat to Coalition Forces in Iraq," Washington Institute for Near East Policy, *Policywatch* no. 827, January 15, 2004, http://www.washingtoninstitute.org/templateC05.php?CID=1705.

105. "Iran's Role in the Recent Uprising in Iraq"; see also A. William Samii, ed., "Thousands of Iranians to Visit Iraq Every Day," *Radio Free Europe/Radio Liberty Iran Report* 6, no. 48 (2003).

106. Kathleen Ridolfo, "Is Iraq Slipping towards Civil War?" *Radio Free Europe/Radio Liberty Iraq Report* 7, no. 6 (2004).

107. Ali Nourizadeh, "Former Iranian Intelligence Officer: Tehran Is Deploying Its Agents in Iraq from North to South," *Al-Sharq al-Awsat* (London), April 3, 2004, http://www.profound.com.

108. Lathem and Dan, "Iran, Hezbollah Aid Crazed Cleric." Notably, this number matches exactly the figure provided in a similar report that appeared in the British Arab-language daily *Al-Sharq al-Awsat* on April 9, 2004.

109. Cited in A. William Samii, ed., "IRGC Commander Discusses New Strategy," *Radio Free Europe/Radio Liberty Iran Report* 7, no. 38 (2004).

110. United States Department of Energy, Energy Information Administration, "Country Analysis Brief: Iran," April 2004, http://www.eia.doe.gov/emeu/cabs/iran.html.

111. Ibid.

112. Ibid.

113. Robin Wright, "Iran's New Alliance with China Could Cost U.S. Leverage," *Washington Post*, November 17, 2004, A21.

114. Energy Information Administration, "Country Analysis Brief: Iran."

Chapter 4

1. "Iran Reinforces Navy after Azerbaijan Beefs Up Caspian Defense, Expert Says," *Ekho* (Baku), April 7, 2004, http://www.lexis-nexis.com.

2. Glenn E. Curtis, ed., *Russia: A Country Study,* 1st ed. (Washington: Library of Congress, 1998), 30; *Iran: A Country Study* (Washington: American University, 1978), 45.

3. *Iran: A Country Study,* 45.

4. See, for example, Bruce Clark and Anatol Lieven, "U.S., Turkey and Iran Chase Power in Central Asia," *Times* (London), February 17, 1992, http://www.lexis-nexis.com.

5. Iranian jurist Ayatollah Abdulkarim Musavi Ardebili, as cited in Martin Marris, "Azerbaijan Termed 'Ripe' for Islam," Associated Press, January 27, 1990.

6. Ibid.

7. See Mohammad Mohaddessin, *Islamic Fundamentalism: The New Global Threat* (Washington: Seven Locks Press, 1993), 67–70.

8. Mohiaddin Mesbahi, "Iran and Tajikistan," in Alvin Z. Rubinstein and Oles M. Smolansky, eds., *Regional Power Rivalries in the New Eurasia: Russia, Turkey, and Iran* (Armonk, NY: M.E. Sharpe, 1995), 120.

9. *Narodnaia Gazeta* (Moscow), July 18, 1992, as cited in Mohiaddin Mesbahi, "Iran and Tajikistan," 120.

10. See, for example, then–CIA Director R. James Woolsey's testimony before the Senate Select Committee on Intelligence on January 25, 1994, http://www.lexis-nexis.com.

11. Mesbahi, "Iran and Tajikistan," 120.

12. "Rafsanjani Sees Regional Grouping as 'World Power,'" Associated Press, February 16, 1992.

13. "Iran Courts Muslim Republics," *Middle East Defense News* 5, no. 8, January 20, 1992, http://www.lexis-nexis.com.

14. "Nazarbayev Receives Iranian Delegation," Itar-TASS (Moscow), November 28, 1991, http://www.lexis-nexis.com; "Iranian Foreign Minister's Visits to Kazakhstan and Kyrgyzstan," *Kyrgyz Radio* (Bishkek), November

28, 1991, http://www.lexis-nexis.com; "Rafsanjani to Turkmenistan," *Middle East Defense News* 5, no. 20, July 20, 1992, http://www.lexis-nexis.com.

15. Ze'ev Wolfson, *Armenian "Traces" in the Proliferation of Russian Weapons in Iran* (Shaarei Tikva, Israel: Ariel Center for Policy Research, December 2002), 25.

16. Brenda Shaffer, *Iran's Role in the South Caucasus and Caspian Region: Diverging Views of the U.S. and Europe* (Berlin: Stiftung Wissenschaft und Politik, July 2003), 3.

17. See, for example, Rowan Scarborough, "Tale Told of How Iran Nearly Got Nuke Gear," *Washington Times*, November 2, 1996, A3.

18. *Times* (London), February 17, 1992, as cited in Mohaddessin, *Islamic Fundamentalism*, 67.

19. Mark Katz, "Russia and Iran: Who Is Strong-Arming Whom?" *Radio Free Europe/Radio Liberty Newsline* 8, no. 131 (2004).

20. Ariel Cohen, "The Primakov Doctrine: Russia's Zero-Sum Game with the United States," Heritage Foundation, *FYI* no. 167, December 15, 1997, http://www.heritage.org.

21. John P. Hannah, "Evolving Russian Attitudes toward Iran," in Patrick Clawson, ed., *Iran's Strategic Capabilities and Intentions* (Washington: National Defense University, April 1994), 56.

22. Ivan Matveychuk, "Moscow-Teheran: Concurrence of Interests: The Iranian Factor and Russo-American Relations," *Voyenno-Promyshlennyy Kuryer* (Moscow), February 25, 2004 (author's collection).

23. *Snark*, Yerevan, 10 August 1999, http://wnc.fedworld.gov.

24. "Iran Shows the Flag in the South Caucasus," *Jamestown Foundation Monitor* 7, Iss. 142 (2001), http://jamestown.org/publications_details.php?volume_id=24&issue_id=2071&article_id=18575.

25. Elizabeth Wishnick, *Strategic Consequences of the Iraq War: U.S. Security Interests in Central Asia Reassessed* (Carlisle, PA: U.S. Army War College, May 2004), 2–4.
26. Jacquelyn Davis and Michael Sweeney, *Central Asia in U.S. Strategy and Operational Planning: Where Do We Go from Here?* (Cambridge, MA: Institute for Foreign Policy Analysis, February 2004), 47.
27. Wishnick, *Strategic Consequences of the Iraq War*, 2.
28. U.S. Department of Defense, *Nuclear Posture Review*, December 31, 2001, http://www.globalsecurity.org/wmd/library/policy/dod/npr.htm.
29. "A military structured to deter massive Cold War–era armies must be transformed to focus more on how an adversary might fight rather than where or when a war might occur." White House, Office of the Press Secretary, *National Security Strategy of the United States of America*, September 2002, 29.
30. U.S. Department of Defense, Office of the Secretary of Defense, *Annual Report to the President and the Congress*, 2002, http://www.defenselink.mil/execsec/adr2002/index.htm.
31. Undersecretary of Defense for Policy Douglas J. Feith, "Transforming the Global Defense Posture," remarks before the Center for Strategic and International Studies, Washington, DC, December 3, 2003, http://www.csis.org/features/031203feith.pdf.
32. "Caucasian Security Discussed," Itar-TASS (Moscow), April 29, 2003, http://www.lexis-nexis.com.
33. A. William Samii, ed., "Yerevan's 'Complimentary Approach' Angers Tehran," *Radio Free Europe/Radio Liberty Iran Report 5*, no. 36 (2002).
34. "Iranian, Armenian Defence Ministers Discuss Regional Security Issues," IRNA (Tehran), March 5, 2002, http://www.profound.com; "Armenia, Iran Sign Military Cooperation Accord," Arminfo (Yerevan), March 5, 2002, http://www.profound.com.

35. "Cooperation of Armenia and Iran in Energy and Transport Sector to Have Positive Effect on Whole Region–Iranian President," ARKA (Yerevan), September 8, 2004, http://www.profound.com.
36. Armenian Foreign Minister Vartan Oskanian, as cited in Shaffer, *Iran's Role in the South Caucasus and Caspian Region*, 13.
37. "Moscow Prepares to Step Up Arms Sales to Turkmenistan," *Nezavisimaya Gazeta* (Moscow), November 12, 2003, http://www.lexis-nexis.com.
38. *Voice of the Islamic Republic of Iran* (Tehran), November 14, 2003, http://www.profound.com.
39. Sergei Sokut, "Rossiyskiy otvet Amerike [Russia's Answer to America]," *Nezavisimoye Voyennoye Obozreniye* (Moscow), October 5, 2001, http://nvo.ng.ru/wars/2001-10-05/1_answer.html.
40. Valery Agarkov, "Iran Concerned over Non-Regional Forces in Two CIS Regions," Itar-TASS (Moscow), August 27, 2004, http://www.lexis-nexis.com.
41. "Russian, Iranian Foreign Ministers Reaffirm Regional Partnership on Terror," *RIA-Novosti* (Moscow), October 10, 2004, http://www.lexis-nexis.com; Vadim Lagutin, "Russian FM Holding Talks in Iran, Discusses Caspian, Nuclear Cooperation," Itar-TASS (Moscow), October 11, 2004, http://www.lexis-nexis.com; "Rowhani, Lavrov Stress Iran's Right to Use Peaceful Nuclear," IRNA (Tehran), October 11, 2004, http://www.lexis-nexis.com.
42. "Russia Reaffirms Continued Nuclear Cooperation with Iran," IRNA (Tehran), December 27, 2004, http://www.irna.ir/?SAB=OK&LANG=EN&PART=_NEWS&TYPE=PO&id=20041227175846F07; "Iranian President Calls Opinion Exchange between Russia and Iran on Nuclear Energy Issues Positive," *RIA-Novosti* (Moscow), December 13, 2004, http://www.lexis-nexis.com.

43. "IRGC Commander Warns Iran Will 'Powerfully Protect' Its Interests in Caspian," ISNA (Tehran), October 12, 2004, http://www.profound.com.

44. For a compelling overview of this competition, see Lutz Kleveman, *The New Great Game: Blood and Oil in Central Asia*. (New York: Atlantic Monthly Press, 2003).

45. Ariel Cohen, "Iran's Claim over Caspian Sea Resources Threaten Energy Security," Heritage Foundation, *Backgrounder* no. 1582, September 5, 2002, http://www.heritage.org/Research/MiddleEast/bg1582.cfm.

46. Scheduled to come online in 2005, the BTC, when fully operational, will be able to carry up to one million barrels of crude per day from the Caspian to Western markets. It will do so by bypassing both Russia and Iran.

47. "Iran, Armenia Sign Agreement on Gas Export," *Asia Pulse*, May 18, 2004, http://www.lexis-nexis.com.

48. Safa Haeri, "Georgian President Calls for Expanded Relations with Iran," Iran Press Service, March 10, 2004, http://www.iran-press-service.com/ips/articles-2004/march/iran_georga_10304.shtml.

49. "Georgia Interested in Gas via Iran-Armenia Pipeline," *Tehran Times*, July 27, 2004, http://www.profound.com; "Georgia Agrees to Buy Iranian Gas," Interfax (Moscow), July 12, 2004, http://www.profound.com.

50. "Iranians, Tajiks Ink Preliminary Agreements," *Radio Free Europe/Radio Liberty Newsline* 8, no. 174 (2004); "Iran to Allocate $150Mln for Tajik Hydroelectric Power Plant," Interfax (Moscow), September 13, 2004, http://www.profound.com.

51. "Iran, Kazakhstan to Set Joint Transport Company," Interfax (Moscow), April 29, 2004, http://www.profound.com.

52. During an October 2003 visit to Tehran, Russian Deputy Foreign Minister Vyacheslav Trubnikov held

closed-door consultations with Iranian Foreign Minister Kamal Kharrazi and Hasan Rowhani, Secretary of Iran's Supreme National Security Council. One result of the wide-ranging discussions, which covered the situations in Iraq and Afghanistan, was a significant stride toward the coordination of Russian and Iranian energy policies, with both countries agreeing to work to keep global oil prices between $25–28 per barrel and to collaborate on maintaining security in the energy-rich Caspian region. *Voice of the Islamic Republic Radio 1* (Tehran), October 12, 2003, http://www.profound.com.

53. In October 2004, Iran's special envoy to the Caspian, Mehdi Safari, huddled with officials in Moscow over a joint stance on foreign involvement in the energy-rich region. The result was a bilateral communiqué opposing "the presence of countries not part of the region of the Caspian Sea." "Teheran Doesn't Want Outside Countries in Caspian Affairs," Interfax (Moscow), October 29, 2004, http://www.profound.com.

54. "Russia Favors Iran Route for Crude Exports," *Tehran Times*, June 14, 2004, http://www.profound.com.

55. "Army Chief Says No Country Can Dictate to Caspian Sea Littoral States," IRNA (Tehran), May 30, 2001, http://www.profound.com.

56. For a summary of this incident, see "A Rogue State's Conduct in the Caspian," *Jamestown Foundation Monitor 7*, issue 143 (2001), http://jamestown.org/publications_details.php?volume_id=24&issue_id=2072&article_id=18581.

57. Mekhman Gafarly, "Bomb with an Oil Fuse," *Defense and Security*, October 24, 2003, http://www.lexis-nexis.com.

58. "Iran Reinforces Navy after Azerbaijan Beefs Up Caspian Defense, Expert Says."

59. "Iran Deploys Ballistic Missile from Sea Vessel," *Middle East Newsline*, October 14, 2004 (author's collection).

60. Glenn E. Curtis, *Russia: A Country Study* (Washington: Library of Congress, 1998), 30.
61. Sevindzh Abdullayeva and Viktor Shulman, "Azerbaijan Marks Azerbaijanis Solidarity Day," Itar-TASS (Moscow), December 31, 2001, http://www.lexis-nexis.com; "Iran," *CIA World Factbook*, http://www.cia.gov/cia/publications /factbook/index.htm.
62. Hanna Yousef Freij, "State Interests vs. the Umma: Iranian Policy in Central Asia," *Middle East Journal* 50, no. 1 (1996), 71–84.
63. Until they were closed down in March 2004, for example, both the Iranian embassy in Baku and its Cultural Center there had for years been funneling money to a number of mosques, and dispensing personal "donations" to their imams. Malahat Rzayeva, "Official to Stop Iranian Donations to Azeri Clergy," *Sarq* (Baku), March 12, 2004, http://www.lexis-nexis.com.
64. These fears have only been exacerbated by a renewed surge of nationalist rhetoric emanating from Baku, which has dubbed "the unification of Azeris living abroad" to be "one of the most important components of the country's policy." "Azerbaijan Marks Azerbaijanis Solidarity Day."
65. Yegana Mammadova, "Iran Is Financing the Islamic Party of Azerbaijan," *Bizim Asr* (Baku), August 6, 2002, http://www.lexis-nexis.com.
66. Ibid.; *Zerkalo* (Baku), April 20, 2004, http://www .lexis-nexis.com.
67. This activity, and the "anti-Azerbaijani propaganda" contained in the broadcasts, led Azerbaijan's Foreign Minister, Vilayet Guliev, to take the unexpected step of issuing an official cease and desist order to Tehran's envoy to Azerbaijan, Ahmed Qazai, in late 2003. "Azerbaijani Foreign Minister Urges Iran to End Broadcasts into Southern Azerbaijan," *Radio Free Europe/Radio Liberty Newsline* 7, no. 204 (2003).

68. Michael Mainville, "Mosque, Carpet Museum, Mosque . . . ," *Gazette* (Montreal), March 22, 2004, A20.

69. "Azerbaijan Will Not Tolerate Religious Extremism: President," Agence France Presse, July 23, 2002.

70. "Iran Moving Ethnic Azeris from Border Districts," *Zerkalo* (Baku), July 31, 2003, http://www.lexis-nexis .com.

71. "Iran Is Gathering Troops on Border with Azerbaijan," *Uch Nogta* (Baku), October 22, 2003 (author's collection).

72. "Iran and Azerbaijan to Sign Religious Cooperation Agreement," IRNA (Tehran), June 22, 2004, http://www .lexis-nexis.com.

73. "Relations Between Azerbaijan and Iran Get Stronger," Azertag (Baku), October 2, 2004, http://www .azertag.com; "Kazakh President, Iranian Security Secretary Discuss Terrorism, Caspian Status," *Khabar Television* (Almaty), October 11, 2004, http://www.pro-found.com.

74. "The Special Services of the Republic of Azerbaijan and Iran Have Signed Three Protocols," *Turan* (Baku), December 20, 2004, http://www.profound.com; Sevindzh Abdullayeva and Viktor Shulman, "Azerbaijan, Iran DefMin to Discuss Mil Cooperation, Security," Itar-TASS (Moscow), December 22, 2004, http://www .profound.com.

75. Cited in Gareth M. Winrow, "Turkish Policy toward Central Asia and the Transcaucasus," in Alan Makovsky and Sabri Sayari, eds., *Turkey's New World: Changing Dynamics in Turkish Foreign Policy* (Washington: Washington Institute for Near East Policy, 2000), 117.

76. Mohaddessin, *Islamic Fundamentalism*, 77.

77. According to statistics from the Turkish Ministry of Foreign Affairs, http://www.mfa.gov.tr/grupa/an/ policy.htm.

78. "Turkey Asks Iran to Lower Gas Price," *Middle East Newsline*, July 29, 2004, http://menewsline.com/stories/2004/july/07_30_4.html.
79. In 2003, bilateral trade between Iran and Turkey increased almost 90 percent from 2002 levels, topping $2.3 billion dollars. Moreover, commerce between the two countries is expected to more than double in the next two to three years, reaching or surpassing $5 billion by 2007. See "Tehran-Ankara Trade Balance in Iran's Favor in 2003," IRNA (Tehran), February 28, 2004, http://www.lexis-nexis.com, and "Volume of Iran-Turkey Trade Exchange up to 1.6 Billion Dollars," IRNA (Tehran), October 3, 2004, http://www.lexis-nexis.com.
80. Umit Enginsoy and Burak Ege Bekdil, "Turkey-Iran Pact Irks United States," *Defense News*, August 9, 2004, 6.
81. Bill Gertz, "Terrorists Trained by Iran Tracked from Uzbekistan," *Washington Times*, April 8, 2002, A01.
82. Ibid.

Chapter 5

1. As Minister of Culture and Islamic Guidance in the mid- to late-1980s, Khatami had been credited with loosening governmental constraints on art, media, and music.
2. "Transcript of Interview with Iranian President Mohammed Khatami," CNN, January 7, 1998, http://www.cnn.com/WORLD/9801/07/iran/interview.html.
3. Secretary of State Madeleine K. Albright, remarks at the Asia Society Dinner, New York, NY, June 17, 1998, http://www.lexis-nexis.com.
4. *Iran and Libya Sanctions Act of 1996*, Public Law 104-172, August 5, 1996, http://www.mipt.org/pdf/iranandlibyasanction104-172.pdf.
5. Ibid.

6. Secretary of State Madeleine K. Albright, statement on "Iran and Libya Sanctions Act (ILSA): Decision in the South Pars Case," London, United Kingdom, May 18, 1998, http://asm.stanford.edu/external/raw/Cryptome031800/dos-spars.htm.

7. Ralph Danheisser, "House Approves Iran Missile Sanctions Aimed at Russian Firms," *Washington File*, June 10, 1998, http://www.fas.org/news/russia/1998/98061001_ppo.html.

8. "Text: Clinton Vetoes Iran Missile Proliferation Sanctions Act," *Washington File*, June 24, 1998, http://www.fas.org/news/iran/1998/98062401_npo.html.

9. Matthew Rice, "Clinton Signs 'Iran Nonproliferation Act,'" *Arms Control Today*, April 2000, http://www.armscontrol.org/act/2000_04/irnap00.asp.

10. Jane Perlez and James Risen, "Clinton Seeks an Opening in Iran, But Efforts Have Been Rebuffed," *New York Times*, December 3, 1999, 1.

11. Louis Freeh, "American Justice for Our Khobar Heroes," *Wall Street Journal*, May 20, 2003, http://online.wsj.com.

12. Dariush Zahedi, *The Iranian Revolution, Then and Now: Indicators of Regime Instability* (Boulder: Westview Press, 2001), 105.

13. See Reuel Marc Gerecht, "Iran: Fundamentalism and Reform," in Robert Kagan and William Kristol, eds. *Present Dangers: Crisis and Opportunity in American Foreign and Defense Policy* (San Francisco: Encounter Books, 2000), 111–45.

14. President George W. Bush, State of the Union address, Washington, DC, January 29, 2002, http://frwebgate.access.gpo.gov/cgi-bin/getdoc.cgi?dbname=2002_presidential_documents&docid=pd04fe02_txt-11.

15. See, for example, "Iran Reacts with Anger to Bush Remark about 'Axis of Evil,'" Deutche Presse-Agentur, January 30, 2002.

16. White House, Office of the Press Secretary, "Statement by the President," July 12, 2002, http://www.whitehouse .gov/news/releases/2002/07/20020712-9.html.
17. Zalmay Khalilzad, "Where Is Iran—and U.S. Iran Policy—Heading?" remarks before the Washington Institute for Near East Policy, Washington, DC, August 2, 2002, http://www.washingtoninstitute.org/pubs/ speakers/khalilzad.htm.
18. Robin Wright, "The U.S. Now Views Iran in More Favorable Light," *Los Angeles Times*, February 14, 2003, http://www.latimes.com/news/nationworld/nation/ wire/la-fg-usiran14feb14,1,4416504.story.
19. The most recent manifestation of this reasoning is *Iran: Time for a New Approach* (New York: Council on Foreign Relations, July 2004).
20. Johannes Reissner, "Europe and Iran: Critical Dialogue," in Richard N. Haass and Meghan L. O'Sullivan, eds., *Honey and Vinegar: Incentives, Sanctions and Foreign Policy* (Washington: Brookings Institution Press, 2000), 42; see also Geoffrey Kemp, "The United States, Europe & Iran: The Ingredients for U.S.-European Policy," remarks at the American Institute for Contemporary German Studies and Johns Hopkins University conference on *The Iranian Dilemma: Challenges for German and American Foreign Policy*, Washington, DC, April 21, 1997, http://www.aicgs.org/Publications/PDF/iran.pdf.
21. Eric Reginald Lubbock Avebury and Robert Wilkinson, *Iran: State of Terror: An Account of Terrorist Assassinations by Iranian Agents* (London: Parliamentary Human Rights Group, 1996).
22. "EU to Open Trade, Political Talks with Iran," Xinhua News Agency, December 12, 2002, http://www.lexis-nexis.com.
23. Stephen Fidler, "Iran Centrifuge Plan Dashes Hopes of Nuclear Deal," *Financial Times* (London), June 25, 2004, http://www.lexis-nexis.com.

24. Glenn Kessler and Walter Pincus, "One Step Forward, Direction Uncertain; U.S. Notes Iran's Cooperation in Iraq War," *Washington Post*, April 18, 2003, A28.
25. Deputy Secretary of State Richard L. Armitage, "U.S. Policy and Iran," testimony before the Senate Foreign Relations Committee, October 28, 2003, http://foreign.senate.gov/testimony/2003/ArmitageTestimony031028.pdf.
26. See, for example, A. William Samii, ed., "Guardians Council Vetting Sets Off Storm of Protest," *Radio Free Europe/Radio Liberty Iran Report* 7, No. 2 (2004).
27. Marc Champion and Carla Ann Robbins, "EU Believes Iran Is 5 or 6 Years from Atom Bomb," *Wall Street Journal*, November 10, 2004, http://online.wsj.com.
28. Ibid.

Chapter 6

1. Iranian officials summarily rejected such proposals when they were floated in the fall of 2004, both by the European Union and by American Democratic presidential challenger Senator John Kerry. See, for example, Eli Lake, "Iran Mocks Kerry's Idea for a Deal on Uranium," *New York Sun*, October 4, 2004, 1.
2. See, for example, "Secretary of Iran's Supreme Security Council, Hassan Rowhani: The World Must Accept Iran's Membership in the World Nuclear Club," Middle East Media Research Institute, *Special Dispatch* No. 678, March 11, 2004, http://www.memri.org/bin/articles.cgi?Page=countries&Area=iran&ID=SP67804.
3. For a comprehensive and lucid retelling of the Osiraq raid, see Rodger W. Claire, *Raid on the Sun: Inside Israel's Secret Campaign That Denied Saddam the Bomb* (New York: Broadway Books, 2004).
4. Michael Eisenstadt, "The Challenges of U.S. Preventative Military Action," in Henry Sokolski and Patrick Clawson,

eds., *Checking Iran's Nuclear Ambitions* (Carlisle, PA: U.S. Army War College, Strategic Studies Institute, 2004), 113.

5. James Fallows, "Will Iran Be Next?" *The Atlantic Monthly* 294, no. 5 (2004), 108.

6. White House, Office of the Press Secretary, *National Security Strategy of the United States of America*, September 2002, 15.

7. As cited in Daniel Sneider, "'Chatter' Hints at Strike on Iran's Nuclear Sites," *San Jose Mercury News*, November 7, 2004, http://www.mercurynews.com/mld/mercurynews/news/opinion/10121646.htm?1c.

8. "Iran's Nuke Program Threatens the Existence of Israel," Agence France Presse, November 17, 2003.

9. See, for example, "Israel Expanding Missile Defense Capabilities, Defense Official Says," *Global Security Newswire*, October 20, 2003, http://www.nti.org/d_newswire/issues/2003/10/20/9c962204-0434-47ee-87a2-bf798769c80b.html; Amos Harel, "Israel, U.S. Conduct Successful Test of Arrow Missile," *Ha'aretz* (Tel Aviv), July 30, 2004, http://www.haaretz.com/hasen/spages/458075.html.

10. Dan Williams, "Israel Seeks More Submarines for 'Strategic Depth,'" Reuters, January 1, 2004; "Israeli Navy Says Its Subs Are Ultimate Deterrent: Presumed Nuclear Force," *National Post* (Toronto), January 2, 2004, A16.

11. Israel has placed priority emphasis on the acquisition of long-range strike aircraft in recent years, and now boasts 62 F-15, 25 F-15I and 203 F-16 multi-role fighters (with deliveries of a scheduled 103 F-16I war planes now underway). However, Israel's contingent of 25 F-15Is are the only planes capable of traversing the estimated 1,500 kilometers to strike Iranian nuclear assets without extensive refueling *en route*. See International

Institute of Strategic Studies, *The Military Balance, 2003–2004* (Oxford: Oxford University Press, 2003), 112, and Kenneth M. Pollack, *The Persian Puzzle: The Conflict between Iran and America* (New York: Random House, 2004), 394. Israel has also commenced amassing "bunker buster" munitions capable of penetrating hardened and buried targets, including Iranian nuclear facilities. In September of 2004, it acquired some 500 BLU-109 advanced laser- and satellite-guided munitions—capable of penetrating close to eight feet of solid concrete, and of being delivered at long stand-off ranges—as part of its annual military aid allocation from the United States. Anton La Guardia, "Israel Challenges Iran's Nuclear Ambitions," *Daily Telegraph* (London), September 22, 2004, 12.

12. Fallows, "Will Iran Be Next?" 108.

13. "Turkey no longer considers countries a threat to each other," Hilmi Ozkok, Chief of the Turkish General Staff, announced in a November 2004 public address before Istanbul's prestigious War Academy. Instead, according to Ozkok, the Turkish government now "attribute[s] first priority to terrorism on the list of contemporary threats to peace and stability in the world." Umit Enginsoy and Burak Ege Bekdil, "Turkey Says Terror, Not Neighbors, Top Threat to the Nation," *Defense News*, November 22, 2004, 4.

14. "Ankara Is Averse to Military Operation," *Sabah* (Istanbul), November 20, 2004, http://www.profound.com.

15. Arieh O'Sullivan, "'Little Israel' Will Not Save World from Iran," *Jerusalem Post*, August 26, 2004, 4.

16. Uri Dan, "Ariel Defends His Axis of Good," *New York Post*, October 1, 2004, 28.

17. As Lt.-Gen. Moshe Ya'alon, the Chief of Staff of the Israeli Defense Forces, has made clear, both Israel and the West need to be prepared to use "other options"

against Iran's nuclear program, should diplomacy fail. Cited in Arieh O'Sullivan, "Ya'alon: We Must Be Prepared to Strike Iran," *Jerusalem Post*, December 13, 2004, 2.

18. President George W. Bush, remarks to the people of Poland, Wawel Royal Castle, Krakow, Poland, May 31, 2003, http://www.whitehouse.gov/news/releases/2003/05/20030531-2.html.

19. Robin Wright, "Seizure Helped Speed Libyan Cooperation on Weapons," *Washington Post*, January 4, 2003, A18.

20. President George W. Bush, remarks on Weapons of Mass Destruction Proliferation, Fort Lesley J. McNair—National Defense University, Washington, DC, February 11, 2004, http://www.whitehouse.gov/news/releases/2004/02/20040211-4.html.

21. Ibid.

22. "United States Signs Agreement with Azerbaijan to Help Ex-Soviet Republic Strengthen Its Borders," Associated Press, January 3, 2004; "Azerbaijan, U.S. Sign Agreement on WMD," *Radio Free Europe/Radio Liberty Newsline* 8, no. 2 (2004).

23. Sevindzh Abdullayeva and Victor Shulman, "U.S., Azerbaijan Begin 10-Day Naval Exercises," Itar-TASS (Moscow), January 26, 2004, http://www.lexisnexis.com.

24. See, for example, Rauf Mirkadyrov and Igor Plugatarev, "US Military Bases Will Appear in Azerbaijan," *Nezavisimaya Gazeta* (Moscow), August 18, 2004, http://www.lexis-nexis.com; Fariz Ismailzade, "US Troop Redeployment Sparks Speculation on Azerbaijani Base," *Eurasia Insight*, August 23, 2004, http://www.eurasianet.org/departments/insight/articles/eav082304.shtml.

25. "Kazakhstan Building Military Base on Caspian with U.S. Help," *Radio Free Europe/Radio Liberty Newsline* 7, no. 191 (2003).

26. Roger McDermott, "Kazakhstan's Western Military Cooperation Sparks Tensions with Russia," *Eurasia Daily Monitor* 1, no. 50 (2004), http://www.jamestown .org/publications_details.php?volume_id=401&issue_id =3014&article_id=2368236.

27. See, for example, "Kyrgyz President Meets with U.S. Centcom Commander," *Radio Free Europe/Radio Liberty Newsline* 8, no. 143 (2004), and "Armenia, U.S. Discuss Military Cooperation," *Radio Free Europe/ Radio Liberty Newsline* 8, no. 78 (2004).

28. For Azerbaijan in particular, the initiatives underway as part of Caspian Guard are a boon, allowing officials in Baku to more effectively combat Iran's clandestine efforts at destabilization in their country.

29. Vladimir Socor, "The Guns of Summer: Iran Prowls the Caspian," *Wall Street Journal Europe*, August 3, 2001, 7.

30. Uzi Rubin, "The Growing Role of Sea-Based Missile Defenses in the Middle East," remarks before the American Foreign Policy Council's Missile Defense Roundtable, July 27, 2004.

31. *Al-Sharq Al-Awsat* (London), October 8, 2003. as cited in "Al-Sharq Al-Awsat Editor: Iran's Nuclear Weapons a Threat to Arab and Islamic Countries," Middle East Media Research Institute, *Special Dispatch* No. 586, October 10, 2003, http://memri.org/bin/articles.cgi? Page=countries&Area=iran&ID=SP58603.

32. See, for example, "Interview: Maj. Gen. Khaled Al Bu-Ainain," *Defense News*, December 1, 2003, 46.

33. Riad Kahwaji, "GCC-U.S. Joint Exercises Tackle Missile Defense," *Defense News*, June 14, 2004, 30.

34. "UAE Evaluates Missile Defense System," *Middle East Newsline*, 10 July 2003, http://www.menewsline.com/ stories/2003/september/09_12_1.html.

35. "Kuwait Considers Air Defense Project," *Middle East Newsline*, November 17, 2003, http:/ www.menewsline .com/stories/2003/november/11_17_2.html.

36. "Bahrain Introducing Patriot Missiles to Reinforce Defense," Deutche Presse-Agentur, January 26, 2003; "U.S. to Sell BMD Radar to Bahrain," *Geostrategy-Direct*, June 3, 2004, http://www.geostrategy-direct.com/geostrategy-direct/secure/2004/6_08/mi.asp?.

37. For more on existing defense ties between the United States and the Gulf states, as well as the potential for their expansion, see Simon Henderson, *The New Pillar: Conservative Arab Gulf States and U.S. Strategy* (Washington: Washington Institute for Near East Policy, 2003).

38. Notably, a number of proposals for such a "Middle East NATO" have already been aired. See, for example, Kenneth Pollack, "Securing the Gulf," *Foreign Affairs*, July–August 2003, 2–15.

39. Vasily Lata and Anton Khlopkov, "Iran: raketno-yadernaya zagadka dlya Rossii [Iran: A Missile and Nuclear Enigma for Russia]," *Yadderny Kontrol* No. 2 (Summer 2003), 39–56.

40. See, for example, Duma Defense Committee Chairman (and former Deputy Defense Minister) Andrei Kokoshin's comments on *Ekho Moskvy* Radio (Moscow), June 3, 2003, http://www.profound.com.

41. "Iran to Develop Joint Fields Whatever the New Iraq Thinks," *worldtribune.com*, June 11, 2004, http://216.26.163.62/2004/me_iran_06_09.html.

42. Ariel Cohen, "Russia and the Axis of Evil: Money, Ambition and U.S. Interests," statement before the House of Representatives Committee on International Relations, February 26, 2003, http://wwwc.house.gov/international_relations/108/85339.pdf.

43. Ibid.

44. See, for example, Martin Walker, "Kurd PM: French, Russians to Lose Iraqi Oil," United Press International, March 14, 2003.

45. Howard LaFranchi, "Turks Pitch In: New Troops to Iraq," *Christian Science Monitor*, October 8, 2003, 01.

46. See, for example, "Turkey Opens Ports, Military Bases to the US for Iraq Reconstruction," *Hurriyet* (Istanbul), June 26, 2003, http://www.profound.com.
47. See, for example, Soner Cagaptay, "United States and Turkey in 2004: Time to Look North," *Turkish Policy Quarterly* 2, no. 4 (2004).

Chapter 7

1. "Poll on U.S. Ties Rocks Iran," BBC, London, October 2, 2002, http://news.bbc.co.uk/2/hi/middle_east/2294509.stm.
2. Ibid.
3. U.S. Department of State, *Iran Country Report on Human Rights Practice for 2002*, March 2003, http://www.state.gov/g/drl/rls/hrrpt/2002/18276.htm.
4. "1.4m Youths Join Unemployed Population Per Year," Mehr News Agency (Tehran), March 7, 2004, http://www.mehrnews.ir/en/NewsDetail.aspx?NewsID=64033.
5. Paul Klebnikov, "Millionaire Mullahs," *Forbes*, July 21, 2003, http://www.forbes.com/forbes/2003/0721/056_print.html
6. See, for example, Ramin Mostagim, "Corruption Eats into Roots of Society," Inter Press Service, July 15, 2004, http://www.ipsnews.net/new_nota.asp?idnews=24640.
7. "Iran Acknowledges Prostitution," Associated Press, July 6, 2000; U.S. Department of State, *2003 International Narcotics Control Strategy Report*, March 2004, http://www.state.gov/g/inl/rls/nrcrpt/2003/.
8. See, for example, "Iranian Lawyer Says Closing Down of Some 100 Publications against the Law," ISNA (Tehran), April 25, 2004, http://www.lexis-nexis.com/.
9. Reporters Without Borders, *Annual Report on Iran*, May 5, 2004, http://www.rsf.org.
10. "A Sorry Election," *The Economist*, February 23, 2004, http://www.economist.com/agenda/displayStory.cfm?story_id=2456871.

11. "UN Chides Iran over Human Rights," BBC, December 21, 2004, http://news.bbc.co.uk/2/hi/middle_east/4114621.stm

12. "Text of Ayatollah Taheri's Letter," *Norooz* (Tehran), July 10, 2002, http://www.daneshjoo.org/article/publish/printer_20.shtml

13. See "Iranian Intellectual: 'Religious Tyranny Is Based on a Fascist Interpretation of Faith . . . Muslims Should Reform Religious . . . Accept Democracy,'" Middle East Media Research Institute, *Special Dispatch,* no. 738, July 2, 2004, http://www.memri.org/bin/articles.cgi.?Page=countries&Area=iran&ID=SP73804; See also "Iranian Intellectuals against Khamenei—Dr. Qassem Sa'idi: 'Your Regime Is Illegitimate, Your Foreign and Domestic Policies Are Failing and Despotic,'" Middle East Media Research Institute, *Inquiry and Analysis* no. 125, February 28, 2003, http://www.memri.org/bin/articles.cgi?Area=reform&ID=IA12503.

14. *Al-Sharq al-Awsat* (London), February 18, 2003, as translated in "Top Iranian Defector on Iran's Collaboration with Iraq, North Korea, Al-Qai'da, and Hizbullah," Middle East Media Research Institute, *Special Dispatch* no. 473, February 21, 2003, http://www.memri.org/bin/articles.cgi?Page=countries&Area=iran&ID=SP47303.

15. "Iran Recruits Arabs for Security Crackdown," *Middle East Newsline*, August 4, 2002, http://www.menewsline.com/stories/2002/august/08_06_2.html.

16. "Countdown to Counter-Revolution," *The Economist*, January 15, 2004, http://www.economist.com/agenda/PrinterFriendly.cfm?Story_ID=2346384.

17. Joe Klein, "Letter from Tehran: Shadow Land," *New Yorker*, February 18, 2002, http://www.newyorker.com/fact/content/?020218fa_FACT.

18. See, for example, "Khamenei Reads Riot Act to Iran Reformers," Agence France Presse, November 12, 2002.

19. Mohammad Mohaddessin, *Enemies of the Ayatollahs: The Iranian Opposition's War on Islamic Fundamentalism* (London: Zed Books, 2004), 2.

20. Author's interview with Iranian dissident, Washington, DC, July 2002.

21. Broadcasting Board of Governors, *Radio Farda, New Persian-Language Service to Iran, Launched*, December 19, 2002, http://www.bbg.gov/printerfr.cfm?articleID=53.

22. See, for example, Jesse Helms, "What's 'Pop' in Persian?" *Wall Street Journal*, December 16, 2002, http://online.wsj.com/; Jackson Diehl, "Casey Kasem or Freedom?" *Washington Post*, December 16, 2002, A25.

23. For example, the "Iran Democracy Act" introduced into Congress by Senator Sam Brownback (R-KS) in May of 2003 included provisions for the expansion of funding for governmental outlets such as Radio Farda. Office of Senator Sam Brownback, *Iran Democracy Act Introduced Today*, May 19, 2003, http://brownback.senate.gov/pressapp/record.cfm?id=204017&.

24. Tom Carter, "Castro Regime Jamming U.S. Broadcasts into Iran," *Washington Times*, July 16, 2003, A13.

25. J. Michael Waller, "Iran and Cuba Zap US Satellites," *Insight on the News*, September 1, 2003, 34.

26. Arch Puddington, *Broadcasting Freedom: The Cold War Triumph of Radio Free Europe and Radio Liberty* (Lexington: University of Kentucky Press, 2000), 253–54.

27. Anthony Blinken, "Winning the War of Ideas," *The Washington Quarterly* 25, no. 2 (2002), 105.

28. Puddington, *Broadcasting Freedom*, ix.

29. Advisory Commission for Public Diplomacy Chairman Harold Pachios, remarks at the Newhouse School of Communication at Syracuse University, Syracuse, New York, January 28, 2003, http://www.state.gov/r/adcompd/rls/19104.htm.

30. Author's interviews with public diplomacy experts, Washington, DC, November and December 2004.

31. *Changing Minds, Winning Peace: A New Strategic Direction for U.S. Public Diplomacy in the Arab & Muslim World,* (Washington: Advisory Group on Public Diplomacy for the Arab and Muslim World, October 1, 2003,) 13, http://www.state.gov/documents/organization/24882.pdf.

32. See, for example, *Finding America's Voice: A Strategy for Reinvigorating U.S. Public Diplomacy,* (New York: Council on Foreign Relations, 2003); Stephen Johnson and Helle Dale, "How to Reinvigorate U.S. Public Diplomacy," Heritage Foundation, *Backgrounder* no. 1645, April 2003; and, most recently, U.S. Department of Defense, Office of the Under Secretary of Defense for Acquisition, Technology and Logistics, *Report of the Defense Science Board Task Force on Strategic Communication,* September 2004.

33. Extrapolated from Broadcasting Board of Governors, *Broadcasting to Iran Fact Sheet,* June 16, 2003, and Broadcasting Board of Governors, *BBG Broadcasting to Iran,* January 4, 2005.

34. In 1983, the combined budget (in constant dollars) of the Voice of America and Radio Free Europe/Radio Liberty was $206.6 million—channeled toward a target audience of some 280 million Soviet citizens. See James L. Tyson, *U.S. International Broadcasting and National Security* (New York: National Strategy Information Center, 1983), 150.

35. *Broadcasting to Iran Fact Sheet.*

36. Notably, the original concept for this format was laid out and presented to Congress well before September 11th, and has not been revamped since the start of the War on Terror. See Hansjoerg Beiner, "The Arrival of Radio Farda: International Broadcasting to Iran at a Crossroads," *Middle East Review of International Affairs* 7, no. 1 (2003), 17.

37. Extrapolated from the 1996 Persian Diaspora Census prepared by Iranian Christians International, http://www.farsinet.com/pwo/diaspora.html.

38. *Iran Democracy Act*, S. Res. 1082, 108th Cong., 1st sess. (May 19, 2003). The bill sought to empower the U.S. State Department to "award grants to an eligible entity for the purpose of funding programs and activities to promote a democratic referendum in Iran."

39. Despite serious bipartisan support, Brownback's initiative was eviscerated during deliberations in the Senate, largely at the impetus of Senators Richard Lugar (R-IN) and Joseph Biden (D-DE). The resulting compromise amendment that was ultimately inserted into the State Department foreign relations authorization bill for 2004 was devoid of any earmarked funds for private broadcasting initiatives. See Editorial, "Ayatollah Lugar," *New York Sun*, July 10, 2003, 6.

40. Johnson and Dale, "How to Reinvigorate U.S. Public Diplomacy," 4.

41. Pahlavi clearly spells out his political objectives in his book, *Winds of Change: The Future of Democracy in Iran* (Washington: Regnery Publishing, 2002).

42. Scott Peterson, "Why the US Granted 'Protected' Status to Iranian Terrorists," *Christian Science Monitor*, July 29, 2004, 7.

43. White House, Office of the Press Secretary, *National Security Strategy of the United States of America*, September 2002, 9.

44. S. Rob Sobhani, "The Prospects for Regime Change in Iran," in Sokolski and Clawson, eds., *Checking Iran's Nuclear Ambitions*, 63.

Conclusion

1. "Text of Agreement between the E3/EU and Iran," Mehr News Agency (Tehran), November 14, 2004, http://www

.globalsecurity.org/wmd/library/news/iran/2004/iran-041114-eu-iran-agreement.htm.

2. European Union foreign Affairs Minister Javier Solana, as cited in Safa Haeri, "Iran—EU's Big 3 Announces Agreement," Iran Press Service, November 15, 2004, http://www.iran-press-service.com/ips/articles2004/november/iran_iaea-nuclear_151104.shtml.

3. "EU, Iran to Resume TCA Negotiations Next Week," IRNA (Tehran), January 8, 2005, http://www.payvand.com/news/05/jan/1071.html.

4. Haeri, "Iran—EU's Big 3 Announces Agreement."

5. Michael Adler, "Iran Still Buying Centrifuge Parts Abroad—Intelligence Officials," Agence France Presse, September 9, 2004.

6. Peter Conradi, "Iran 'Has Secret Nuclear Lab,'" *Sunday Times* (London), November 28, 2004, 20.

7. Louis Charbonneau, "Iran Wants Guarantee of No 'Regime Change'—Diplomats," Reuters, October 15, 2004.

8. Elaine Sciolino, "UN Action Frustrates U.S. on Iran," *International Herald Tribune*, November 30, 2004, 1.

9. "Iran Boasts 'Great Victory' over US, Warns Nuclear Freeze Is Temporary," Agence France Presse, November 30, 2004.

Index

Page numbers in *italics* refer to figures and tables.